Creating an Excellent Salon

A Guide to Business Practice for NVQ Level 3 and Higher Qualifications

IRIS RIGAZZI-TARLING

2nd Edition

With additional interviews and self assessments by Frances Franklin

Hodder & Stoughton

A MEMBER OF THE HODDER HEADLINE GROUP

Dedication

For my mother, May

Orders: please contact Bookpoint Ltd, 78 Milton Park, Abingdon, Oxon OX14 4TD. Telephone: (44) 01235 827720, Fax: (44) 01235 400454. Lines are open from 9.00–6.00, Monday to Saturday, with a 24 hour message answering service. Email address: orders@bookpoint.co.uk

British Library Cataloguing in Publication Data
A catalogue record for this title is available from The British Library

ISBN 0 340 772 972

Second edition 2000
First published 1994
Impression number   10 9   8   7   6   5   4   3   2   1
Year   2005 2004 2003 2002 2001 2000

Copyright © 2000 Iris Rigazzi-Tarling

Typeset by Wearset, Boldon, Tyne and Wear.
Printed in Great Britain for Hodder & Stoughton Educational, a division of Hodder Headline Plc, 338 Euston Road, London NW1 3BH by J.W. Arrowsmith Ltd., Bristol

Contents

Preface

Creating an Excellent Salon has been revised to include all the current legislation and business practice that is essential for running a business. The book is intended for **all** students and post-graduate students studying Beauty Therapy and in particular for **anyone** who wants to improve their skills in:

- personal management
- leadership
- training and appraisal
- marketing
- financial and business management

as well as the salon owner or business person seeking to refresh their skills in business practice.

The books structure is **simple** and **concise**. The content includes syllabus criteria for **NVQs** and **SVQs Levels 2 and 3** and major national and international qualifications awarded by:

- C&G
- EDEXCEL (BTEC)
- VAI
- IA
- CIBTAC
- CIDESCO
- ITEC

The emphasis throughout the book is on being **competent**. **Key skill** areas are identified on each chapter to assist the reader with **learning based activities** and **self-assessment** if applicable or for the salon owner the informative text will serve as a vital handbook. The book is designed to be a source of information and useful addresses appear in the text as well as in the back of the book.

Most countries offering courses leading to international qualifications in beauty therapy have laws that are similar to those in Britain in relation to acquiring a business licence, the environment and the payment of taxes. The overseas reader is therefore encouraged to seek all the relevant information as suggested in the book, but in relation to the country in which she is living. This is important because legislation in the USA, Australia and South Africa is different from state to state. In Europe it varies from country to country and the practice of beauty/body therapy can be restricted because of medical legislation.

The use of 'she' throughout the text is the author's choice, to simplify writing.

Introduction

Where do **you** want to be in 3 years time, 5 years or even 10?

Your long-term targets and short-term goals are important. Industry demands that you know what you want and how you're going to achieve it.

So – have you set your goals? Is management for you or are you aiming to own your own business?

The beauty industry demands a variety of technical skills and people skills and a very high standard of professional expertise if you are to be successful, because there is a lot of competition out there in the marketplace.

This updated text is designed to help you develop your personal management skills and gain insights into effective leadership and salon ownership so that you have the essential ingredients to establish yourself and be successful. Only you can supply the drive and motivation to achieve your goals.

Be positive, be focused and be successful.

Key skills for NVQ

Key skill areas have been identified on each chapter opening page to enable the student to be aware of the skill areas available. The activities are designed to offer opportunities to gather evidence for portfolios. **The six key skills are:**

Communication	**C**	Problem Solving	**PS**
Application of Number	**AN**	Improve own Learning and Performance	**IOLP**
Information Technology	**IT**	Working with Others	**WWO**

I wish to thank all my colleagues in Beauty Therapy and the students and clients for their assistance in updating this book.

I would like to thank the interviewees for their valuable contribution, Sheila Lewis for her specialist advice on the accountancy section and John Cragg, Director of IPTI, for his assistance with the latest insurance information.

Finally, my grateful thanks to my husband Nick, who typed the manuscript.

The author and publishers would like to thank the following for permission to reproduce photographs in this book: Ellisons, Taylor Reesen, the Runnymede Hotel and Health and Beauty magazine.

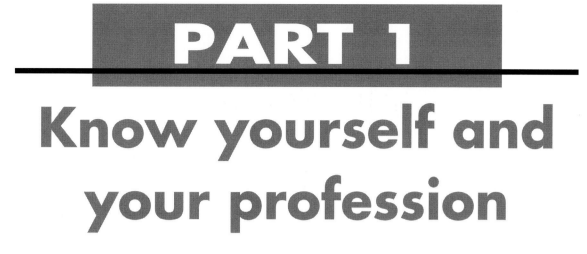

PART 1

Know yourself and your profession

CHAPTER 1

Know yourself

OBJECTIVES

Knowing yourself will help you to make correct choices concerning your work and your future. Self-evaluation, knowing your strengths and weaknesses, and identifying your needs, personality type and values will help you to see yourself as the character you really are and to project yourself as the person you want to be and help you to be successful.

Life is constantly changing and so you will need to adjust and change. In order to achieve your aims, set short-term targets to be realistic and to mark your achievement. You will need to evaluate your performance on a regular basis if you really want to know yourself, and be successful.

It is vital if you are going to operate a successful business that you first know yourself. When you are able to evaluate yourself and know your strengths and weaknesses, you will be able to identify your needs and discern strengths and weaknesses in your colleagues. There are certain key areas:

Identify

your character type	your strengths and weaknesses	your values	your aims

These will help you to:

 Know yourself and plan your future.

STRENGTHS AND WEAKNESSES

 What type of person are you? Are you:

self-motivating	caring
honest	enthusiastic
smart	friendly
willing	self-reliant
ambitious	patient
hard-working	sympathetic
self-confident	energetic
strong	competent

CHARACTER TYPE

What do you like doing

Do you enjoy: using your imagination

creating new ideas
|
forward planning
|
trusting in a chance idea
|

If so, you are:

CREATIVE

|

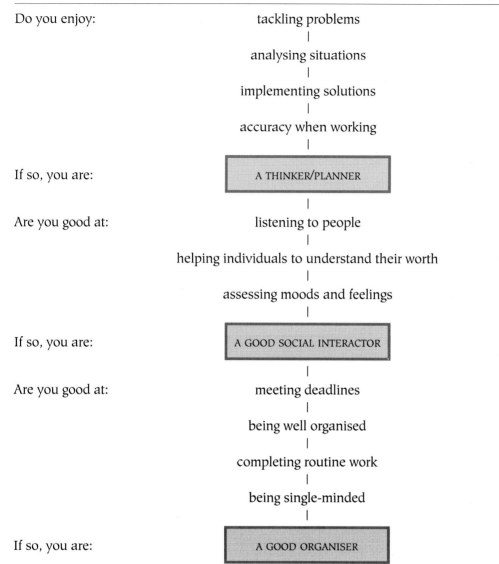

Do you enjoy:

tackling problems
|
analysing situations
|
implementing solutions
|
accuracy when working
|

If so, you are:

A THINKER/PLANNER
|

Are you good at:

listening to people
|
helping individuals to understand their worth
|
assessing moods and feelings
|

If so, you are:

A GOOD SOCIAL INTERACTOR
|

Are you good at:

meeting deadlines
|
being well organised
|
completing routine work
|
being single-minded
|

If so, you are:

A GOOD ORGANISER

Fortunately, as we are all individuals we do not fit into one 'box-type'. We often find we have more than one major quality. This is when a knowledge of our own values can assist us.

VALUES

Analysing **your values** and adding them to your **natural strengths** and aptitudes helps you to begin a happy and successful career. Once you have decided on **your own goals**, you aim for them.

Do you value:

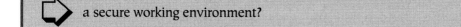

a secure working environment?

If so, look for a position with a **regular routine**, closely defined duties and a regular wage and benefits.

Do you value:

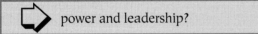

freedom and flexibility?

Would you like your working environment to be casual and relaxed with shifts or flexitime? Would you **value** being able to use your own initiative?

Do you value:

achievement?

If so you must set your aims at **short-term goals**, and you must work in a situation where your achievement is recognised and rewarded.

Do you value:

financial success?

If you aim to achieve **a good income**, you must be prepared to go for high salaries and lots of perks. You must have plenty of skills and be competent and determined.

Do you value:

power and leadership?

If you want **power and leadership** – to be the best and to arrive at the top – you must look for a working environment that gives you plenty of experience and opportunities to succeed.

Do you value:

people?

Working closely with colleagues and having time to talk to clients can make your working life a pleasure. **Good communication skills** and a friendly working environment are sometimes lost in the busy, non-stop pressure of a high-powered business. You must decide on the 'right' work-place.

AIMS

Once you have identified your aptitudes and values, you are able to identify your aims and set goals.

 Short-term targets are best if you are to be successful. Your aims will also be governed by the type of image you intend to project.

 Will you be a **confident, smart, knowledgeable, reliable optimist?**

Will you build your reputation on your skills and personal qualities? What will *you* do?

Self Assessments and Activities

1 What type of person are you?

List your *personal* qualities.

2 Identify your character type(s).

(a) Are you an organiser or a thinker?

Are you a creative person?

Are you a social interactor?

Answer:

(b) Make a list of your strengths and weaknesses.

3 What are your values?

(a) Do you value security?

(b) Do you value freedom and flexibility?

(c) Do you value financial success?

(d) Do you value power and leadership?

(e) Do you value achievement?

(f) Do you value people?

Place these in order of importance to you.

4 Your aims.

How will you decide on your aims?

Answer:

5 Why is it important to 'know yourself'?

Answer:

When you have completed this section you will have successfully made your first evaluation.

1 List the transferable skills that you have that could be used in the Beauty Industry.

2 Identify your personal weaknesses and strengths then give examples on how you would cope with them in the salon environment.

3 'Being a professional' – what does it mean to you? Explain your answer.

4 Write a personal profile to be included in your portfolio. Give reference to your personal qualities and any relevant experience you have gained prior to commencing your course.

CHAPTER 2

Know your profession

OBJECTIVES

This chapter explains the importance of holding recognised qualifications in beauty therapy and in being a professional. The major associations set the standards for the professionals. Professional standards start with your personal standards. These can never be too high. When qualified, membership of an association will give you status and professional 'back up'. Finally, when you apply for a position you will need to prepare a CV. This is your passport into work and needs regular updating as you progress in your career. The skills-based CV and speculative letter enhance your opportunities.

RECOGNISED QUALIFICATIONS

If you want to be successful in your work you must:

■ know your trade or profession; and
■ be professional.

You must hold qualifications that are recognised in this country, and if you intend to work overseas, your qualifications must have international status. Recognised qualifications mean that **you**:

 have followed a professional training of a specified length

have learnt the practical and theoretical skills demanded for your chosen career in beauty therapy.

MAJOR AWARDING BODIES

Most FE/state colleges and private schools take the examinations of one or more of the major awarding bodies. Major examining boards offer similar qualifications and most of these are of international status or are recognised by international associations for membership.

Edexcel (BTEC)
Stewart House
32 Russell Square
WC1B 5DN

City and Guilds London Institute
46 Britannia Street
London WC1 9RG

Confederation of International Beauty Therapy and Cosmetology
Parabola House
Parabola Road
Cheltenham
Gloucestershire
GL50 3AH

International Aestheticiennes
Bache Hall
Bache Hall Estate
Chester CH2 2BR

International Therapy Examination Council
10–11 Heathfield Terrace
Chiswick
London W4 4JE

Scottish Vocational Authority
Hanover House
24 Douglas Street
Glasgow G2 7NQ

Vocational Awards International/Vocational Training Charitable Trust
46 Aldwyck Road
Bognor Regis
PO21 2PN

GOOD PRACTICAL AND THEORETICAL SKILLS

In addition to holding a recognised qualification, you will need to be experienced in all your practical and theoretical skills. You will also need to be **numerate** and **demonstrate good written language**.

PERSONAL MANAGEMENT SKILLS

If you are going to be successful you must learn how to manage **yourself**, your **time** and your **aims**.

TIME MANAGEMENT

So, how do you know if you are effective at managing your time?

A simple **self-assessment** will help you to identify if you have a problem. Complete the self-assessment **and list the main points that you will need to address**. Effective leadership means that you know how to manage your time.

SELF ASSESSMENT – TIME MANAGEMENT Tick List	Yes	No
1. Am I a time waster?		
2. Do I waste other peoples time?		
3. Do I put off doing things?		
4. Do I manage my time?		
5. Do I set deadlines?		
6. Do I meet deadlines?		
7. Do I plan my tasks?		
8. Do I spend too long on a task?		
9. Do I delegate tasks?		
10. Am I a perfectionist?		
11. Do I prioritise tasks – put them in order?		
12. Do others control my time?		
13. Do I control my time?		
14. Do I have a clear idea of what I want to achieve each day?		

When you have listed the main points that you need to change suggest ways to do this and make an **action plan** to help you achieve your aim.

Effective use of **TIME** means:

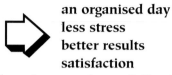

an organised day
less stress
better results
satisfaction

In order to **manage your time** you will need to complete a **daily timesheet** so you can assess how you spend your day.

A daily timesheet could look like this:

TIME	ACTIVITY
7.00am	Get up – go to bathroom
7.30am	Coffee/breakfast
7.45am	Get dressed
8.00am	
8.15am	
↕	
23.30pm	
24.00pm	

It is necessary to complete a whole day accurately so that you can assess what you do. Then you might prepare a **daysheet planner** in order to **plan** your tasks and a timescale for completing them.

Regular practice of a **daysheet** will improve your **personal planning time management**.

This **method** is often used in business **to assess the needs** of a salon/establishment, and your staff can monitor this.

When you **manage yourself** and your time effectively you usually achieve your **aims**. In order to achieve your **aims** or goals you will need to set **targets**.

Aims/goals

These are necessary if you want to focus your efforts and ideas and make definite plans. When you manage your time effectively goals can become a reality.

Goals can help you solve problems or prevent problems

In order for goals to be achievable they should contain a time scale

|

be under your control

|

be realistic

|

have a definite outcome

Some goals my be **short-term**: i.e. tomorrow or next week. Other goals may be **long-term**: i.e. next year or 3 years time.

Whatever your goal you will need to set **targets**. This makes it easier to monitor success as you progress and it makes your goal **more** achievable.

When setting your goals it is always a good idea to build in a **contingency plan**. This means that you have considered **alternatives** to your goal and a **flexible approach** ensures that there is less chance of your goal being unattainable.

Regular evaluation of yourself will ensure that you are on the right track and that you will **develop your aims** and **manage your time** well.

REMEMBER

 You can help your staff achieve their **goals** and be successful as well.

BEING A PROFESSIONAL

Professionalism and a good personal code of ethics are acquired by following a professional training. The term 'professional' is used often, but what does it mean to the beauty therapist? It means that there are many ways in which she must demonstrate her professional skills.

Be a **professional** from the start

in appearance
with colleagues
to clients
in attitude and service

Appearance means

a clean, ironed, smart uniform
low-heeled, clean shoes that fit securely
good, all over personal hygiene
short, clean, well-manicured, unvarnished nails

light day make-up

hair off the face, an appropriate length, well groomed and clean

no jewellery except a wedding band and small earrings

always present a good self-image

With colleagues means:

never gossip

always ensure open lines of communication

discuss problems, never criticise

never poach clients

always maintain accurate records to assist colleagues

be flexible, approachable, co-operative

With clients means:

always communicate effectively

ensure confidentially at all times

never make claims or promises about your services

always display a list of your charges

only advertise within your limits

always hold full insurance cover

always ensure the client records are accurate and that the client has accurate written information on home-care

In attitude and service means

treat everyone the same irrespective of nationality, religion or social class

be respectful, understanding and helpful

always give your undivided attention

listen to client's problems, do not talk about your own

give honest, knowledgeable and accurate advice

always use language your clients understand

always be in control

always be reliable and responsible

PROFESSIONAL ASSOCIATIONS

When you adopt a professional approach to your work, you are demonstrating the standards of your industry. You will want to join a **Professional Association** so that you have the trademark of a **professional** and a stamp of approval for the public and the industry.

 Membership of an Association means:

- a membership badge and certificate;
- insurance cover;
- business advice;
- regular newsletters;
- meetings to update your technical knowledge.

CODE OF ETHICS

All **professional associations** have their own **code of ethics**. They have a world-wide standard to maintain and members are usually required to sign a declaration that they will abide by the **Code of Ethics** to ensure that the **standards of their profession** are upheld. For a list of major associations see page 195.

Below is a typical code of ethics of an international association.

Code of Ethics

The Independent Professional Therapists International, hereinafter referred to as I.P.T.I. or the Association, require that all members without regard to grade, status or position should at all times maintain the highest level of professional conduct.

THE CODE is intended to help establish what is appropriate and acceptable practice and to protect members of the public from improper practices.

THE CODE is also intended to help maintain honourable standards of behaviour of members, towards each other, towards clients and members of the public and toward other professional institutions and their members.

THE CODE is not intended to place restrictions on individual members but does place a member under obligation to his profession and professional body.

1. A member must always act with due regard to the laws, customs and practices of the country in which he or she works.
2. A member shall practice only within the limits of his professional training and competency.
3. A member shall not treat any person who to his knowledge could be suffering from any condition likely to be affected by the treament without the knowledge and consent of the person's medical practitioner.
4. A member who suspects a client is affected by any condition medical or otherwise beyond the range of his training must decline treatment and advise the client to consult an appropriately qualified practitioner.
5. Membership incurs an obligation to uphold the dignity and honour of the profession, to exalt its standing and to extend its usefulness to the public. The conduct of members shall at all times be both becoming and creditable to the profession.
6. A member should always act professionally towards clients and fellow practitioners, should maintain secrecy and confidentiality in his work and not criticise the work of a fellow practitioner.
7. No member shall for any reason offer treatments, aid or advice to any person known to be under the care of another member of I.P.T.I. without the consent of such member.
8. A member temporarily taking charge of a client of another member shall make no effort to influence such client to leave his usual therapist and shall uphold as far as is consistently possible and shall in no way disparage the methods of any such member. In consultation due regard shall be paid to the therapist in charge of the case.
9. A member who has been employed as an assistant by another member shall not at the termination of his employment or on the decease of his former employer where the practice of his former employer has been purchased by another member circularise or otherwise attempt to induce clients to forsake the practice of such former employer.
10. All duly constituted medical bodies shall be respected and endeavours made to merit the esteem of medical practitioners with whom members may come into contact.
11. The fact of clients changing to another therapist or another setting up in practice near at hand should not be allowed to influence the friendly relationship which should exist among all members.
12. A member may use the appropriate designatory letters on letterheads and in advertisements and publicity providing that the placement and content of such advertising material always conforms to the high standards of professional practice without hint or reference to any form of impropriety.
13. In cases where a member acts jointly with or practices in partnership with one or more persons (whether they are all members of the Association or not) they shall not use the designatory letters of the Association after their joint names or after the title of the firm or in any manner directly or indirectly calculated to lead to the assumption that all such persons are individually all members of the Association.
14. Any member who resigns membership or permits their membership to lapse may not display the Association certificate and must cease all use of the Association's designatory letters, logo and other devices.

TREATMENT OF CLIENTS BY THERAPISTS OF THE OPPOSITE SEX
In some clinics and salons it is necessary and accepted that treatments be given by therapists on clients of the opposite sex. In such situations a strictly professional approach must be adopted. There shall be no unnecessary disrobing of the client and the therapist shall be properly dressed to avoid any provocation. It is desirable that a third person be on hand and that the treatment cubicle be accessible.

DISCIPLINE
All members are subject to the Association's Code of Ethics.

The Association reserves the right to investigate any reported incident of misconduct or breach of the Association's Code of Ethics and to take whatever action it deems to be appropriate in the interest of the Association and the Profession at large.

In enforcing the Code of Ethics and subsidiary ethical rules and in endeavouring to prevent improper practices being performed by persons other than our members we depend on the co-operation of all members. If members learn of breaches of the code or know of establishments permitting activities which reflect upon and lower the status of our profession and bring our work into disrepute then they should report such matters in writing. All such reports will be treated in the strictest confidence.

INDEPENDENT PROFESSIONAL THERAPISTS INTERNATIONAL, 58A BRIDGEGATE, RETFORD, NOTTS DN22 7UZ

Figure 2.1 IPTI code of ethics

PRODUCING A CURRICULUM VITAE

When applying for a position, your employer will want to know:

your educational background

 your skills

your work experience

The outline of your educational and professional history is called a **curriculum vitae** (CV) and is presented in a **particular way**. The sample opposite will help you to create your own CV:

Your completed CV should be typed/word processed for easy reading and good presentation. It should have a clear, concise layout. It is a good idea to produce several copies.

 Your CV should be updated regularly so that all your achievements are recorded.

Many employers send a **formal application form** when you apply for a position. This may record the information in a similar way to your CV. You should complete the **application form** and return it with a **letter of application**.

Many beauty therapists choose to make an application for a job even if there is not a position being advertised. This direct approach means that the beauty therapist can think about the type of organisation where she would like to work. She can send a CV and speculative letter to the various companies and ask that the CV is retained on their files for future reference.

This practice is very common and employers like to maintain a recruitment file.

If you want *your* CV to be retained make sure that it is:

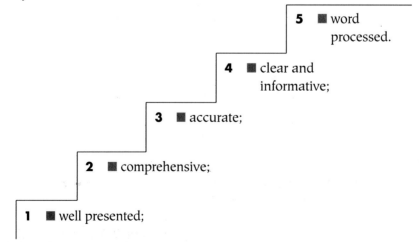

5 ■ word processed.

4 ■ clear and informative;

3 ■ accurate;

2 ■ comprehensive;

1 ■ well presented;

CURRICULUM VITAE

Name: Anne Other

Date of birth: 07.09.80

Address: 72 Any Road, Anytown, Herts, HRS QSZ
Telephone no: . . . .

Marital status: Single

Car driver: Full licence

School/further   Peaks Comprehensive
education   Natler Road
                  Anytown
                  September 1991 – July 1998

                  Anytown FE College,
                  Anytown
                  September 1998 – July 2000

Examinations: GCSE   Passes   Grade
June 1998   English Language   A
                  English Literature   B
                  French   B
                  History   A
                  Biology   B
                  Physics   C
                  Art   B

                  'A' Level
                  English   B

July 2000   City and Guilds
                  Certificate in Beauty Therapy
                  Certificate in Electrolysis

Work experience: Debenhams Department Store
                  Anytown
                  Two weeks April 1998

Interests/hobbies: Swimming, reading, dancing

References: Mrs R Scott, Head Teacher,
                  Peaks Comprehensive School,
                  Anytown (former head teacher)

                  Mr P Maitland, The Manager,
                  Debenhams Department Store,
                  Anytown (former employer)

Figure 2.2 Sample curriculum vitae

After a few years in employment you may choose to design an additional CV which is **skills-based**. This has become increasingly popular and is often used to accompany a speculative letter.

SPECULATIVE LETTER

12 Any Close
Sampletown
Middlesex TW15 3AE
Tel. 01784 863436
25 January 2000

Ann Leader
Human Resources Manager
Head Office
Best Salons
Anytown
London

Dear Ms Leader

I am a mature, confident and out-going person seeking a position in management and I am writing to enquire about possible employment in your organisation.

You will see from my CV that I have the necessary skills and I am keen to progress to a large, expanding company.

I would welcome the opportunity to meet with you, to discuss how my skills could benefit your business.

I look forward to hearing from you.

Yours sincerely

Jane Sample

Curriculum Vitae

Jane Sample
12 Any Close
Sampletown
Middlesex TW15 3AE
Tel. 01784 863436

I am a good organiser and effective communicator, I have a proven track record as a therapist, sales promoter and assistant manager. I am now seeking a position in which my management skills can be fully developed.

Key skills
- efficient and reliable
- experienced beauty therapist
- effective leader
- self-motivator, works well under pressure
- friendly with a good sense of humour

Previous experience
Nov 1997   Beautiful Salon, Sampletown, London.
            Assistant Manager responsible for the daily running of a busy salon with six therapists, sales promotions and some staff training.
Sept 1996–97 Health and Leisure Spa, Oxford
            Beauty Therapist, exercise instructor team leader.

Education and training
Sept 1986–93 Reelands School, Sampletown
            5 GCSE's including Maths, Biology and English and 'A' level English
Sept 1993–96 Reelands Further Education College, Sampletown
            BTEC National Diploma, Beauty Therapy/Epilation
            ITEC Aromatherapy and Reflexology

Interests ....

References ....

Self Assessments and Activities

1 Make a list of at least 12 points that you consider to be important qualities as a professional beauty therapist.

2 In sub-groups discuss how important each of the following is to you:

    a) travelling distance;

    b) salary;

    c) weekend working;

    d) friendly colleagues;

3 State the benefits of belonging to a professional organisation.

4 Look through a trade journal, select three jobs that appeal to you and prepare a letter of application to each.

5 Prepare your own CV.

6 Describe the professional appearance of a beauty therapist.

7 Make a list of the professional associations you are eligible to join once qualified and apply for an information pack.

8 a) Make a plan of your goals for next year, 3 years' time and 5 years' time.

    b) Prepare a contingency plan to safeguard your interests.

9 Prepare a speculative letter.

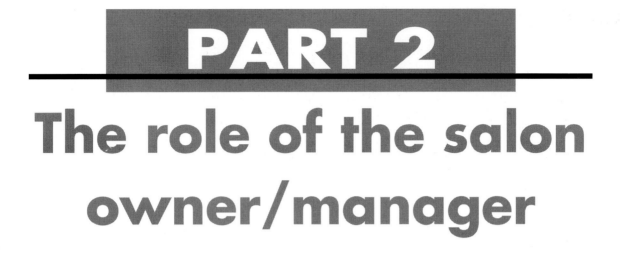

PART 2

The role of the salon owner/manager

CHAPTER 3

Effective Leadership

OBJECTIVES

This chapter explains the importance of good leadership skills for the salon owner. In order to be successful she must be assertive, motivated and organised and be able to work well with people. Effective organisation of the staff and the salon is reflected in an efficient service to your clientele.

GOOD ORGANISATIONAL SKILLS

The salon owner should be able to demonstrate good leadership and good organisational skills by establishing and operating a business with an efficient team of staff.

The salon owner will create a general atmosphere of:

where employees can work in a **stimulated, friendly environment**.

The salon owner will ensure that:

aims and objectives
are clearly defined

|

the employee is able to be
flexible and adjust to change

|

the employee feels secure in
a relatively structured
environment (with a relaxed atmosphere)

Good management/leadership is about employing all the necessary skills so that you can achieve your goals effectively with the support of your staff.

As manager/leader you must be a **thinker**; you will need many skills and as a person you must identify with your own **character type**:

A dynamic person can be too overpowering for employees. She will be full of ideas that she wants carried out immediately. She likes to work under pressure and often creates it for her staff. She will speak her mind and expect results. She enjoys challenges.

A passive person is often too laid back. She is indecisive and does not motivate herself or her staff, by offering very little direction. Situations are left to solve themselves.

An assertive person is the best leader. She

is able to respect herself and others
expresses thoughts honestly and directly and sees the other persons point of view so there is less chance of misunderstanding
is able to deal with situations and reach satisfying solutions
is in control of her life and is decisive and a self-motivator
sees opportunities and acts upon them

What sort of manager/leader **you** are will depend very much on the skills you will need.

The salon owner knows how to manage time efficiently and has effective organisational skills which are transmitted to staff and clients **instantly**.

The effective leader presents

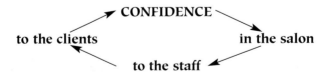

Business is founded on **service**. Reliable, efficient organisation of the salon suggests good **service** and gives staff and clients **confidence** in you.

YOU WILL NEED TO BE	
Organised	prioritise and get the important things done first
Motivated	recognise opportunities and respond to them
Respectful	value the employees' contributions, ask their advice
able to encourage teamwork	check individual 'strengths' encourage decision making
able to delegate and negotiate	give employees tasks which they can do (never delegate tasks that you are not prepared to do yourself)
able to counsel and be patient	listen to the problems of your staff in private, reassure them and help them find a solution
able to offer praise and encouragement	verbal reward for a job well done encourages respect
able to solve problems by evaluation	seeing 'all' sides, able to 'stand back' and objectively assess the situation
efficient	a business runs well if you have sound policies and an organised harmonious atmosphere which encourages staff stability and effective performance.

Figure 3.1 The effective leader

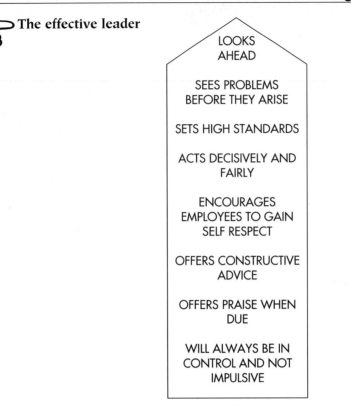

The effective leader

LOOKS
AHEAD

SEES PROBLEMS
BEFORE THEY ARISE

SETS HIGH STANDARDS

ACTS DECISIVELY AND
FAIRLY

ENCOURAGES
EMPLOYEES TO GAIN
SELF RESPECT

OFFERS CONSTRUCTIVE
ADVICE

OFFERS PRAISE WHEN
DUE

WILL ALWAYS BE IN
CONTROL AND NOT
IMPULSIVE

INTERVIEW WITH SARA – TRAINING MANAGER FOR VIRGIN INFLIGHT THERAPISTS

Q: What type of course did you originally take?
I took two courses C&G in Beauty Therapy and Electrical Epilation and a Higher Diploma. This was a two year programme of study way back in 1978! Some years later I also trained with Tisserand in Aromatherapy.

Q: Where did you train?
The London College of Fashion in Oxford Street, London. At the time I trained it was one of the only 3 colleges that offered the Higher Diploma in this country.

Q: What was your initial ambition?
The usual one, I wanted to be a make up artist! I hoped to work for the BBC but that all changed half way through my course, when I fell in love with Electrical Epilation!

Q: What made you go into teaching?
After having my first child, I desperately wanted to get my brain working again, and

teaching gave me the opportunity to do this and work part-time around my family. I already had a wealth of commercial experience which included owning my own salon.

Q: Please give a brief account of your career to date.
I started my career as Manageress of a salon in Launceston, Cornwall, before moving on to open my salon within a Health Club, in the idyllic setting of North Cornwall. Three years later, my husband and I decided to move away and eventually ended up in Brighton where I managed a salon in Haywards Heath. When I started my family I set up as a mobile therapist and completed a FAETC. I was offered some part-time teaching at several colleges. In 1991 I started at Lewes Tertiary College and 8 years later had risen to the dizzy heights of Beauty Coordinator! From there I joined Virgin Touch as Training Manager.

Q: How does a busy lecturer keep up their practical skills?
By helping out friends who own salons. I do this as often as I can or when they are really short staffed! I have also kept up my mobile practice. I also take every opportunity to take further training with companies that supply Virgin.

Q: Tell me more about your job role with Virgin Touch?
Well we have both 'in-flight therapists' and 'salon therapists' in our Upper Class lounges in Heathrow, Gatwick, Boston and our Virgin Hotel in Majorca. Therapists come to us fully qualified but then train in the Virgin techniques. My role is to structure and organise all this training, introducing new training strategies when and where I feel necessary. I also carry out appraisals on the training staff. I monitor the training in the salons abroad, and organise promotional talks to colleges.

Q: It sounds like a fantastic job opportunity, is there a down side?
No, really – I love my job! The only thing I could think of is the travelling to and from my office but I use this as 'my time', space for myself before putting on my 'housewife' hat!

Q: What are your immediate career plans?
To stay where I am for a while! My job is varied and challenging and I really enjoy it. I also work with some really nice people. Long term, I would love my own training school but we'll have to wait and see.

Q: How will you maintain your practical skills?
I still keep up my mobile work and as an External Verifier I have to keep my skills up to date and therefore I visit exhibitions and attend training courses whenever I can. I also do the occasional treatment for colleagues in the office. As usual we are the last to get anything done!

Q: How much can an inflight therapist expect to earn?
This varies. Staff are paid a basic salary but get either flight allowances, shift pay or

commission depending on where they are based. They also receive an excellent travel package.

Q: What qualities do you look for when selecting an inflight therapist?
A fully recognised qualification, together with at least one years' work experience ideally. More importantly, they need to be friendly and outgoing, able to talk easily to a variety of people and have excellent customer service skills.

Q: Describe the promotional ladder for a successful employee.
Unfortunately the promotional ladder is limited but as Virgin Touch continues to grow, this may change. At the present time she could become an 'in-flight assessor' or possibly join the training team, but the openings are highly sought after!

Q: What skills do you consider makes a good manager?
The ability to listen before making decisions.
Treating your staff with respect.
Flexibility.
Well organised.
Calm.

Q: Do you mind all the travelling? It must be difficult to juggle family commitments.
I love the travelling abroad and have an extremely supportive husband who has been behind me all the way and is perfectly capable of looking after the children when necessary. The kids themselves are really proud of me and think my job is really exciting and this makes it much easier!
I have to be really organised and have the backing of a good team.

Q: What are the perks of your job?
The travelling, the variety of work, the brilliant environment. I have never worked with such a supportive team! Finally, I get to meet all sorts of people including the Stars!

Self Assessments and Activities

1 List the leadership qualities you possess.

2 Describe how you would attempt to develop or improve your leadership skills.

3 State two possible situations (for each) that could arise in the salon which would test your skills:

    as an employer   an organiser

    a delegator   a leader

4 Explain why you believe an assertive person would make a good manager.

5 Imagine you have been working as an assistant manager of a busy salon for 3 years. Explain how you would identify your own training needs.

CHAPTER 4

Staff selection

OBJECTIVES

Staff selection requires managerial skills. You will need to be able to prepare a job description/specification and advertisements and interview applicants. You will need to demonstrate good interviewing techniques if you are to obtain the 'right' staff.

After you have selected and appointed staff, you will need to issue a written statement or contract. There are various contracts that you will need to be familiar with, as well as knowing how to terminate a contract and dismiss staff. Some knowledge of various Acts – Equal Pay Act, the Employment Rights Act 1996, the Sexual Discrimination Acts, the Race Relations Act and the Misrepresentation Act and so on – will provide you with a good background knowledge as an employer.

Staff selection is a managerial task. When selecting staff you will want to employ people who are going to help make your business successful. You will want your staff to be able to perform many duties in addition to looking smart and:

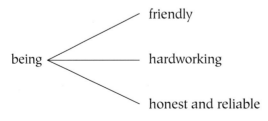

JOB SPECIFICATION

First you will prepare a **job description specification** which will outline:
- the job title;
- the employee's immediate superior;
- the duties and responsibilities;
- the experience and qualifications necessary to fill the position (physical and personal skills);
- the pay and package you will offer.

Next, you will place an advertisement in places where you feel will gain the best response. A professional journal such as *Health & Beauty Salon* would be ideal, but you might like to consider your **local paper**, and **employment agencies**. An advertisement might look like the one below (remember, **you are paying for the size of the advert, so you need to say everything necessary and as briefly as possible**).

Figure 4.1 Health and Beauty Salon magazine

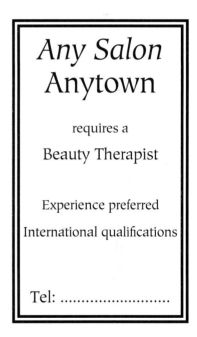

Figure 4.2 Sample simple advertisement

THE INTERVIEW

What to look for

Once you have received applications and CVs you will need to make a list of suitable applicants and then ask them to attend an interview.

Make sure you advise them clearly about the interview:
- the time;
- the place;
- anything they will need to bring, for example, an overall (if you wish to see a demonstration of practical skills).

Interviewing demands a number of skills:

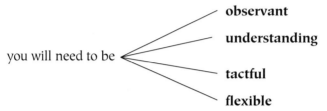

you will need to be
- observant
- understanding
- tactful
- flexible

in order to establish a good rapport.

A good interviewer allows the applicant to talk about herself. You will ask **open questions**, that is, questions which do not imply answers. An example of this could be: '**Tell me about your . . .**', which allows the interviewee to give detailed answers. If you are too rigid or act impatiently, the interviewee will become tense. You should also be aware of the **applicant's non-verbal behaviour**. Are the applicant's actions telling you something different to what is being said?

If the applicant is to demonstrate her skills or abilities and outline her previous experience, **a relaxed, friendly atmosphere is necessary**. The following points should assist you:

The interviewer

should use the CV as a basis for the interview
|
should ask the applicant to expand on certain areas
|
should be led by the applicant's answers
|
should ask open questions
|
should be attentive – and listen to the applicant's replies
|
should check her career aims
|
should establish what motivates her
|
should allow the applicant to ask questions

> The interviewee

should be smartly dressed
|
should be honest
|
should be able to analyse her experience and career aims
|
should be knowledgeable about her work
|
should be asked questions about her skills
|
should ask prepared questions

You may wish to see some applicants a second time before deciding on who to employ. You will need to consider following up references, and should reply as soon as possible to applicants you will not be seeing again.

> Always keep your applications on file – you may wish to refer to them again in the future.

CONTRACTS OF EMPLOYMENT

The Employment Rights Act 1996

Once you have selected staff, you are required by law to give them written terms and conditions of employment – a written statement of employment – within 13 weeks from the date they commenced working for you. (This is not required if the employee works for less than 16 hours per week, or for long-standing employees who have worked 8 hours a week for at least 5 years.) This is not officially a contract and need not be signed by employer or employee to be enforced.

Unwritten contracts

'In law, employees have a contract of employment as soon as they start work even when the written statement of its terms and conditions has not been given to the employee.' Dept. of Employment.

These exist where no formal contract has been made. If the verbal contract is broken, it is often a difficult procedure to prove it, so a formal contract is advisable.

Contract of employment

The contract of employment differs from a statement of employment in that it is usually a **formal agreement** which both the employer and employee sign. Problems can arise with contracts, so it is advisable to have the contract drawn up by a solicitor. The minimum details to include in a contract are:

- name of employer;
- name of employee;
- date employment began;
- title of the job;
- hours of work;
- workplace location;
- rate of pay including overtime, commission and frequency of payment;
- sick pay (terms);
- maternity leave (terms);
- holiday pay;
- holiday entitlement;
- pension information or scheme;
- disciplinary and grievance procedures;
- safety rules;
- length of notice for termination of employment.

There are various types of contracts.

Open-ended contracts

These are for an unspecified period of time and are terminable by either side giving notice as stated in the contract.

Fixed-term contracts

"These are for a certain period of time and will automatically come to an end.

Short-term contracts

These are for three months or less. If the employee is offered repeated short-term contracts, this is regarded by law as continuous employment.

Termination of a contract – The Employment Protection (Consolidation) Act 1978

Employment can be terminated by either party giving the correct notice as stated in the contract. This might not necessarily meet the requirements of current legislation. **The Employment Protection (Consolidation) Act 1978 states that the employer must give:**

one week's notice after four weeks' continuous employment

two weeks' notice after two years

one weeks' notice for each year of continuous employment up to a maximum of twelve weeks if the employee has been with the business for two years.

The employee must give at least:

one week's notice after four weeks' service (unless the contract of employment states otherwise)

the employee's request can be oral or written

the employer must reply within 14 days.

DISMISSING STAFF

When appointing staff, you will no doubt take great care to ensure that you have selected the right people for the position. However, circumstances change and the performance of individual employees may also change. A minor problem, such as lateness, usually shows up on the appraisal form, but if there is no improvement it could be a reason for dismissal.

 Misconduct at work and an inability to do the required work are main reasons for dismissal.

According to the main **Employment Acts**: if dismissal is *fair* there is a certain procedure that must be followed:

 there must be sufficient reason **and** the employer must have acted reasonably

The employee who persists in being late to work cannot be dismissed without warning. This would be **unfair**. In order for the situation to be fair, the employer would have warned her at least three times:

- an informal verbal warning;
- a formal verbal warning;
- a formal written warning;
- a final written warning.

The employer would be given a suitable period to change and correct the matter. Then the dismissal would be fair if there had been no improvement.

Fair dismissal means:

the reason for dismissal has been identified

|

the reason was fair

|

the employer's action was reasonable

Immediate dismissal would be acceptable for **gross misconduct**, for example, stealing.

GRIEVANCE PROCEDURE

You will need to be aware of **Grievance Procedure**.

The employee has rights relating to any grievance which is directly concerned with conditions of employment. **The correct procedure for the employee is to:**

report to the line manager/or supervisor immediately – another employee may accompany her

the matter could be resolved, if not

the grievance must be put in writing and sent to the manager when a formal meeting should be arranged so that the grievance can be fully investigated and resolved.

If this is not the case then outside agencies can be contacted such as ACAS (see page 57).

Your responsibility as the salon owner/manager

You must ensure that the grievance is correctly handled. This means that you must:

have all the necessary information (facts);

hold an interview, as soon as possible to solve the problem;

ensure that any other people involved are contacted;

try and reach a suitable solution that is acceptable to every one, in particular the employee;

all details of the interview should **be recorded in writing** and any **action to be taken** is **recorded and implemented** as soon as possible;

everyone should be satisfied that the result is satisfactory in the working environment.

It is the employer's responsibility to ensure fair dismissal. If the employee is not satisfied, she can take the matter to an employment tribunal. The tribunal then considers whether the employer has followed a discipline which is acceptable to the specifications of the Advisory Conciliation and Arbitration Service (ACAS see page 57).

EMPLOYMENT TRIBUNALS

Industrial Tribunals were renamed Employment Tribunals on 1 August 1998. Responsibility for employment legislation passed in July 1995 to **the Department of Trade and Indus-**

Figure 4.3 Fair and unfair dismissal booklet

try. The Tribunal is a Government approved Body that investigates grievances at work. The Tribunal must try to obtain an agreement between employer and the employee. They have the authority to:

demand re-instatement of the employee
to award financial compensation if re-instatement is not practical

WHY PEOPLE MAY BE UNEMPLOYABLE

The beauty industry demands high standards, hard work and a high degree of skill competency. People who are unemployable in the beauty industry usually present:

———→ inadequate qualifications

————→ poor self-presentation

—————→ a lack of interpersonal skills

Their work references often show that:

performance is poor

|

they are irresponsible

|

they are poor time-keepers

|

they are often unreliable

|

they do not respond to personal counselling

ACTS RELATING TO EMPLOYMENT

You will need to be familiar with parts of certain Acts relating to employment or your solicitor will advise you.

Equality in the workplace is an important factor and the **Equal Pay Act of 1970** and the **Sexual Discrimination Acts of 1975 and 1986** are directly concerned with equality. The Equal Pay Act says that employees who do the **same** work:

- must be employed on the **same** pay; *and*
- must be employed on the **same** terms.

The Sexual Discrimination Acts advise that it is an offence to discriminate between married or unmarried women and men in relation to:

- job advertisement;
- job application;
- job promotion.

The **Race Relations Act 1976** says that as an employer you cannot discriminate against employees on the grounds of colour, race or nationality in recruiting and employment.

The Disability Discrimination Act 1995 prevents the employer, of 20 or more people, from **discriminating** against an existing employee, or a prospective employee, 'the employer has refused to offer or has deliberately not offered him the employment', due to reasons relating to their disability.

This means that **the employer must**:

- make 'reasonable changes to the working environment' if the employee or prospective employee, is proficient/competent to do the job;
- ensure that the employee with a disability/special needs is able to cope in the work-place.

The person entering into a contract is protected by the **Misrepresentation Act 1967**. A claim can be made if a person claims misrepresentation of terms and suffers damage.

The Working Time Regulations 1998 are particularly concerned with:

- the maximum weekly working time;
- patterns of work – night work;
- daily rest;
- weekly rest;
- rest breaks;
- entitlement to annual leave;
- records;
- payment in respect of leave.

They are to **protect the employee** from working too long without sufficient rest time. The employee should be aware that the Regulations stipulate that:

- **the working week should not exceed 48 hours in a 7 day period – averaged over 17 weeks (including overtime)**
- after **6 hours continuous work** employees should have a **rest break** and at least 11 consecutive hours rest break in each **24 hour period** and **35 consecutive hours rest** in any week
- **annual leave entitlement** in any year is **4 weeks** (commenced November 1999)
- records must be kept to show that the limits specified, in **certain** regulations, 'are being complied with in the case of each worker employed by her in relation to whom they apply'.
- these records must be retained for 2 years.

Self Assessments and Activities

1 List the personal qualities that you think are essential for a good manager.

2 List the qualities you would look for when interviewing prospective staff.

3 Design a small advertisement for an experienced therapist and find out what it would cost to place it in a local paper and a professional journal.

4 Prepare a job description for an experienced beauty therapist in a large salon.

5 Make a list of questions you would ask an applicant at an interview.

6 Briefly describe the importance of a written contract of employment;

    (a) for a new member of staff; and

    (b) for the beauty therapist who is leaving.

7 Write a letter to inform an applicant that she/he was unsuccessful in a job application.

8 Make a list of points that might show your employee is unsuitable for the position.

9 Obtain information from ACAS and make a list of the points where ACAS could assist a small business.

10 Explain 'fair dismissal' and its importance to you as an employer.

11 You are a successful salon owner, design an advertisement for your local paper for an experienced therapist.

12 Describe the appropriate attire for an interview.

13 You are interviewing two people for one vacancy (a senior beauty therapist). Plan the agenda.

14 State the objectives of the Disability Discrimination Act 1995.

15 Briefly explain the importance of the written contract of employment for a new member of staff.

16 Explain how would you handle the following situations:

    a) an ex-employee complains she has been unfairly dismissed;

    b) an employee has a personal problem and it is affecting her work.

17 Write a report on a member of staff who is repeatedly late for her early shift. She has received 2 verbal warnings.

CHAPTER 5

Key Skills
C
PS
IOLP
WWO

The law and the salon owner

OBJECTIVES

This chapter deals with the content of some of the major Acts which affect the salon owner – including the Health and Safety Act 1974 – as well as accidents in the workplace and the correct reporting of them, maternity rights, redundancy and redundancy payments.

THE HEALTH AND SAFETY EXECUTIVE

The salon owner has a duty to ensure employees' health and safety in the workplace. She must work within a legal framework.

Government **Legislation** (Acts) and regulations (particular details) mean that the salon owner knows what to do.

The European Union (EU) has had considerable influence on the laws in the U.K. because eventually the EU is working towards a common standard for its members. The EU issues **directives** and member countries produce their **regulations**.

The Health and Safety Executive (HSE)

The HSE enforces health and safety legislation in the U.K. The HSE appoint national inspectors to do this. It is the Local Authorities who send inspectors **Environmental Health Officers**, to visit some business premises and shops, **without notice** at any reasonable time, to check that an employer is working within the law (The Health and Safety (Enforcing Authority) Regulations 1998.

Inspectors can:

- examine the safety, health and welfare aspects of a business;
- investigate an accident or complaint;
- talk to employees;
- take photographs and samples;
- expect co-operation and answers to their questions;
- impound dangerous equipment.

If a problem is found they can:

- issue a formal notice – an **improvement notice** and the employer has a set time, usually 21 days to correct the problem;
- issue a **prohibition notice** which means that the employer must stop the business until all the health and safety problems have been rectified. Failure to comply with this notice could lead to prosecution. The employer may appeal to an **Employment Tribunal** (formerly Industrial).

> ☞ Inspectors have the power to prosecute a business or an individual for breaking Health and Safety Laws

More information can be obtained from
HSE
Rose Court
Southwark Bridge Road
London SE1 9HF

The Health and Safety at Work Act 1974

This is the main Health and Safety Act and all subsequent legislation comes together under this Act. The Act identifies the duties of the employer and the employee in the workplace.

The Act requires:

> the employer to

'so far as is reasonably practicable' safeguard the health, safety and welfare of all her employees.

The employer must provide

a safe place to work, that is:

- **safe** access/egress (exits);
- **safe** equipment;
- **safe** handling;
- **safe** storage;
- **safe** transport of materials; and a
- **safe** healthy environment.

The employer must provide

- **safety information/training and supervision;**
- and publish **a written statement** (if she employs five or more people) of her general policy on health and safety, update it when necessary, and bring it to the attention of her employees.

The employer's duty to other persons

is to ensure, so far as reasonably practicable, that persons not in employment are not exposed to risks to their health and safety; this includes contractors' employees, self-employed persons and the public.

The employee's duty

- is to take reasonable care while at work to avoid injury to herself and others;
- is to assist and cooperate with the employer in meeting the statutory requirements;
- is not to misuse or alter anything that has been provided to ensure her safety.

The Local Government (Miscellaneous Provisions) Act 1982 (Local Authority Licensing)

Local Authorities are responsible for registering Beauty Therapy Businesses. The Environmental Health Officer will inspect your business to ensure that you comply with the law. The law is primarily concerned with hygiene and the safe practice of treatments such as electrical epilation, ear piercing and micro-pigmentation.

To comply with the law:
- the business premises must be registered in order to carry out treatments;
- individual therapists must be registered with the local authority in order to practice.

In order to be registered a salon must have:

- clean premises;
- adequate equipment for the sterilisation of instruments and materials used;
- effective hygiene practices for storing, using and disposing of sharp implements;
- qualified therapists to carry out treatments involving needles.

These regulations are issued by the Local Authority so it is vital to check with your Local Council to ensure you know the exact requirements. If your business meets the requirements you will be issued with a **certificate of registration which must be displayed**.

COSHH 1

The Control of Substances Hazardous to Health Act (COSHH) 1989

This law protects the individual from the exposure of hazardous substances in the workplace. Both the **employer** and the **employee** must be aware of the potential hazard of some substances and the necessary safety precautions that must be taken.

The law requires the employer to:

Assess all the substances which may be hazardous (cleaning materials, beauty products)

Evaluate the harmful effects – the health risks

Determine what needs to be done to reduce the risks

Create rules and regulations which will ensure safe storage handling and use, transportation and disposal of substances

Provide training for all staff on the correct method of use

Regularly monitor the 'control measures', analyse and interpret the results in order to review their effectiveness

Keep all written assessments of control measures

The Health and Safety Executive Publication IND, (G) 136L Revised – A new Brief Guide for Employers assists the employer or delegated person in preparing the assessment of potential hazards by outlining the necessary information/precautions that is required to comply with the law.

Hazardous substances can enter the body by:

the eyes
swallowing
absorption/or a break in the skin
inhalation

Hazardous substances can:

cause skin irritation
allergies
burn the skin
give off fumes
irritate nasal passages
cause breathing difficulties or KILL

KNOW YOUR SUBSTANCES and their **SYMBOLS**
Check health hazard cautions

Figure 5.1 Symbols

Ensure that you have the manufacturers DATA SHEETS on all substances
Handle and store all substances correctly
Dispose of them safely

It is your **responsibility** to ensure that all your products are correctly labelled.
Clients buy products and some substances may be **a health hazard** e.g. nail polish remover.

COSHH (REGULATIONS) 1992

The Environmental Protection Act 1990

This Act deals with the **safe disposal of hazardous substances**, so as not to harm the environment. This Act is linked to the COSHH Act (1989).

EU REGULATIONS 1992 (THE SIX PACK)

The EU Directives on Health and Safety of 1992 incorporated new provisions and became known as **the six pack** because of the six new sections:

1. The Management of Health and Safety at Work Regulations 1992
2. The Workplace (Health, Safety and Welfare) Regulations 1992
3. The Provisions and Use of Work Equipment Regulations 1992
4. The Personal Protective Equipment (PPE) at Work Regulations 1992

5. The Health and Safety (Display Screen Equipment) Regulations 1992
6. The Manual Handling Operations Regulations 1992

The Management of Health and Safety at Work Regulations 1992

The employer has specific duties according to the Work Regulations. The employer's duties to other persons means that the employer must:

consider the risks to health and safety for employees and members of the public and make a written assessment of any risks that may be present

implement appropriate procedures to ensure **preventative measures**

regularly monitor **risk assessments**

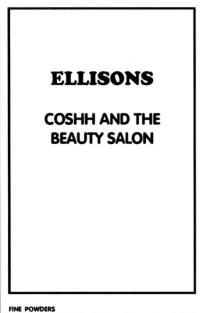

ELLISONS

COSHH AND THE BEAUTY SALON

Health hazard: contact with the eyes will cause damage to the cornea and eyelids; can produce an allergic reaction in sensitive individuals or following excessive exposure to vapourised fluid.

You must read and obey the manufacturers advice printed on the container.

General use/handling guidelines: Keep in a closed, covered container. Avoid breathing in the vapour. Keep off the skin - wear rubber gloves. Thoroughly rinse instruments in warm water to remove all traces of the chemical before use

Storage: Store in a cool dry place.

Disposal: Safe disposal down normal drains if rinsed away with plenty of water. (Empty containers: rinse thoroughly with water and treat as household waste).

Action:

Eye contact:	Contact with the eye will cause damage to the cornea and eyelids. Rinse immediately with plenty of water and continue for 10 to 15 minutes. Seek medical advice.
Skin contact:	Avoid skin contact, will cause skin staining, repeated contact may cause skin sensitisation. Light duty rubber gloves are recommended. Wash contaminated skin. If irritation persists seek medical advice.
Inhalation:	Use in ventilated area. High levels of sustained exposure may cause headache and chest discomfort. Remove to fresh air, seek medical advice if symptoms persist.
Ingestion:	Harmful if swallowed. May cause nausea, vomiting. Drink two glasses of cold water. Induce vomiting and seek medical advice immediately.
Spillage:	Wear gloves and eye goggles, mop up using plenty of water. Maximum ventilation possible.

Always check manufacturers leaflet for any safety updates

FINE POWDERS
Health hazard: inhalation of fine particles can cause irritation

Use/handling: Care should be taken when mixing powders, filing false nails, applying loose powder make-up etc. Avoid making unnecessary dust. Avoid inhaling even in small quantities. If dispensing large quantities of fine powders a face mask is advisable.

Storage: Store in cool dry place in closed container.

Disposal: Treat as domestic waste unless there is a particular hazard e.g. Flowers of sulphur is a fire hazard.

Action:

Eye Contact:	Rinse with plenty of water. If discomfort persists seek medical advice.
Skin contact:	Wash to remove particles. Seek medical advice if any irritation persists.
Inhalation:	Move to fresh air. If coughing and irritation persist seek medical advice.
Ingestion:	Seek medical advice immediately.

Beauty products coming under this category are:

Acrylic Nail Powder	*Bleaches*
Bronzing Powder	*Calamine Powder*
Deodorant Powder	*Face Powder*
Flowers of Sulphur	*Fullers Earth*
Kaolin	*Magnesium Carbonate*
Nail Kits	*Pedicure Talc*
Purified Talc	

Figure 5.2 Data Sheets

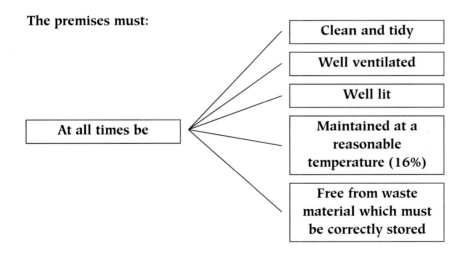

keep a **record** of all **risk assessments**

train employees in all relevant aspects of health and safety

make sure employees have current information on health and safety

display the poster 'Health and Safety Law' and any statutory information on Health and Safety

review health and safety regularly

check employees are properly trained to do their work

keep a record of first aid treatment and injuries

report accidents/diseases and dangerous occurrences (see pages 50–1)

The Workplace (Health, Safety and Welfare) Regulations 1992

These regulations have taken the place of most of the Offices, Shops and Railway Premises Act 1963. The regulations are to ensure that the workplace is a safe and healthy place for every employee and visitor.

These regulations relate to every part of the business premises, from the salon to stairs and passageways.

The premises must:

At all times be →
- Clean and tidy
- Well ventilated
- Well lit
- Maintained at a reasonable temperature (16%)
- Free from waste material which must be correctly stored

- have floors, stairs and passageways that are properly constructed and these must be safe, non-slip, free from obstructions and have properly maintained fixtures and fittings;
- have fire-fighting equipment and fire exits which are accessible and unlocked.

The employer must provide

- clean staff toilets and client toilets, suitably lit, properly ventilated and easily accessible with washing facilities by each toilet;
- washroom facilities must have running hot and cold water, soap and towels (or equivalent) which are well maintained with adequate lighting and ventilation, from windows or another method, fresh air supply system – air conditioning;

- drinking water and drinking utensils (cups);
- an area for the employees' clothing to be hung;
- an area where food and drink can be consumed and resting facilities free from tobacco smoke;
- a changing room for staff who need to change clothes in order to work;
- safe, secure storage for clothing;
- equipment and systems that are in good repair and efficient working order and are regularly checked and repaired when necessary and all testing records are kept.

The Provision and Use of Work Equipment Regulations 1992

These regulations require the employer to ensure that all equipment used in the salon is:

correctly constructed
suitable for its purpose
well maintained, in a good state of repair

The regulations apply to new and second-hand equipment.

The employer must also ensure that:

all **employees** are trained to use the equipment effectively and know how to maintain it
all equipment is serviced on a regular basis
written records are kept of any servicing, repairs or checking of equipment

The Personal Protective Equipment (PPE) at Work Regulations 1992

These regulations deal with selecting, providing, maintaining and using PPE. They require the employer to ensure that any employees who may be exposed to a health risk or injury, is provided with effective protective equipment.

The employer must:
1. **Assess** the need for PPE
2. **Select PPE** that is suitable for the work
3. **Supply** free PPE
4. **Maintain** PPE

The Health and Safety (Display Screen Equipment) Regulations 1992

These regulations are to protect employees who work at Display Screen Equipment, such as Visual Display Units (VDU) attached to a computer. Working at DSE can lead to muscular and other physical problems, eye strain and mental stress.

Minor fatigue is often caused by:

concentrating on the screen for a long time
poor positioning of the DSE
poor lighting including glare and reflections
flickering of the image on the screen

The employer must:

Assess the risks and plan effective ways to deal with them.

This means that employees using DSE should have:

regular breaks and change of task
an adjustable chair to maintain correct height and back support
a display screen where brightness and contrast can be adjusted
regular eye tests which are provided by the employer

Electro Magnetic Radiation

DSE usually emits only low radiation. There is often concern for pregnant women. **The National Radiological Protection Board (NRPB)** '... does not consider such levels to pose a significant risk to health'. Therefore no special protective measures are required.

The Manual Handling Regulations 1992

Injuries can occur by the incorrect lifting of loads and the incorrect lifting and carrying of objects can cause strain, or a major injury can occur after a single incident.

These injuries often result in pain, time off work and sometimes permanent disablement.

The Regulations require the employer to:

Assess the risks to employees of any manual handling tasks:

to assess how risk of injury can be avoided
provide training for all staff on correct manual handling procedures

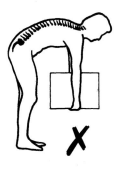
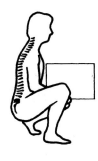
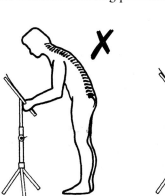

Figure 5.3 Safe lifting and standing

find alternative ways to carry/handle loads

to eliminate the need to manually handle and load equipment by adapting the workplace

The Regulations require the employee to:

'take reasonable care' of their own health and safety and other people

use safe handling methods

use any equipment or systems provided to assist in the safe handling of loads

comply with the Health and Safety Regulations for the workplace and to work with the employer to maintain a safe place to work

The Electricity at Work Regulations 1989/1992

These regulations require a business to

- test all electrical appliances at least once a year (by a qualified electrician);
- Keep the written test sheets (these could be inspected by the Health and Safety Authority).

This testing is commonly known as **PAT** testing (*Portable Appliance Testing*) and a PAT sticker is attached to each appliance after testing and until it is updated. Regular checks should be made to find faults such as:

- frayed or worn wires;
- cracked or loose plugs;
- cracked or damaged equipment casing.

Faulty equipment must be taken out of use immediately and sent for repair.

The Reporting of Injuries, Diseases and Dangerous Occurrences Regulations 1995 (RIDDOR)

These Regulations update the 1985 regulations. They protect the employees and members of the public who may suffer work-place injury and deal with the correct reporting of the incident in an **Accident Book** and if necessary to the **Enforcing Authority** on **RIDDOR Form F2508**.

The simple procedure is this:
- date
- time — of the accident
- place
- full name and occupation of the person
- purpose of visit to the salon
- details of the injury
- course of the accident
- a brief description of the accident
- appropriate action taken
- witness signature (if possible)
- therapist's signature
- salon owner/manager's signature

This must be in an Accident Record Book specifically for this purpose.

The Reporting of Injuries, Diseases and Dangerous Occurrences Regulations 1995 state that employers must notify the enforcing immediately by telephone/fax if a serious accident occurs:

- someone dies
- receives a major injury
- poisoning
- electric shock

A written report form (F2508) must be completed within ten days and sent to the Health and Safety Inspector at the local Enforcement Office.

REMEMBER

- always have copies of the Report Form F2508 available and ready to use for accidents **(for notifiable diseases form F2508a)**

Checkpoints

- deal with any immediate injury/emergency
- make premises safe
- report the accident (if necessary)
- keep all records for at least 3 years

Be Prepared

In all business/establishments

- there should be an action plan
- staff should know what to do

They need to know who:

- will raise alarm
- will control the incident
- will make the premises safe
- are the key people i.e. First Aid Officers

FIRST AID

'All businesses must have an appropriate level of first aid treatment available'. Health and Safety (First Aid) Regulations 1981.

This means for most small businesses that they **must**:

- **Appoint** a trained person to take charge in an emergency and to look after First Aid equipment and there must be one 'appointed person' available when people are working.
- **Provide** and maintain a First Aid Box (see below). The box should contain information/guidance on the treatment of injured people:
  – how to control bleeding;
  – how to give artificial respiration;
  – how to deal with unconsciousness.

■ **Display** notices which state
 – locations of first aid equipment;
 – name of person(s) responsible for First Aid.
■ **Ensure** that the first-aider updates her training.

Some larger businesses require a first aid room and qualified first aiders. Where businesses train first aiders they must be registered through **EMAS** – the **Employment Medical Advisory Service**. Check with your local **Employment Medical Advisor** for details.

REMEMBER

It is the business of **everyone** to know about First Aid

Your First Aid Box

The contents of the box will vary according to the number of staff employed.

There are **basic items** you require:
■ one guidance/information card;
■ individually wrapped sterile adhesive dressings;
■ sterile eye pads with attachments;
■ medium sterile dressings – unmedicated;
■ large sterile dressings – unmedicated;
■ triangular bandages;
■ safety pins;
■ wound cleansing wipes;
■ phials of sterile saline.

Any other **general first aid additions** are an asset, such as:
■ scissors;
■ disposable gloves;
■ gauze;
■ surgical adhesive tape;
■ instant ice sports pack.

Useful Information

Emergency numbers should also be placed in the first aid box, e.g. local health centre, doctor, local hospital, in addition to local emergency services – ambulance, fire, police and so on.

The first aid box should be kept in a **damp-free, dust-free area**. The box must be **green** and clearly marked '**First Aid**', accessible to all members of staff.

The Fire Precautions (Workplace) Regulations 1997

These regulations update the Fire Precautions Act 1971 and Fire Regulations Act 1976.

The Employer's duty is:

to provide a means of escape in case of fire for staff and the public

↓

exits must be marked fire exits and kept closed to prevent a fire from spreading

↓

to ensure that the escape area is kept clear of

↓

obstructions at all times

↓

to ensure the escape area is properly maintained
and all fire fighting equipment is easily available
and properly maintained

↓

to ensure that all employees must be aware of the
escape route and the fire procedure in the event
of a fire and notices for fire evacuation procedure
should be clearly displayed

The Employer must: (if she employs 5 people or more)

Assess fire risks in the workplace
Produce effective ways to deal with them
Provide minimum safety standards
Keep a written record of the risk assessments
Ensure that all employees are aware of the findings

The employer must also ensure that:

there is adequate, correct fire-fighting equipment
smoke alarms or other fire detection equipment
fire doors are fitted
all equipment is checked regularly and kept in good working order
all written records are kept

All staff

> **know how** to raise the alarm
> **are trained** in fire evacuation procedures
> **know where** the fire-fighting equipment is located
> **know how** to use it

Make sure you know which fire extinguishers to use

The **latest** Fire Extinguishers to conform with *BSEN3 Regulations* are all **RED**

Each extinguisher has:

1. **a coloured panel** to show the contents
2. **states the contents**
3. **states the size** (kilograms or litres)

RED = **Water** for wood, paper, textiles

CREAM = **FOAM** for burning liquid, wood, paper, textiles

BLUE = **POWDER** for burning liquid, electrical, wood and textiles

BLACK = **CARBON DIOXIDE** for burning liquid and electrical fires

GREEN = **HALON** for burning liquid and electrical fires (The latter is now obsolete but many may still be in operation)

Other fire-fighting equipment includes a **fire blanket** which can extinguish a small fire.

Fire Prevention in the Business Premises

- Ensure fire alarms are fitted.
- No smoking notices should be displayed throughout the business (industry demands that smoking is discouraged in the workplace).
- Be careful with wet articles e.g. towels and headbands. These should never be placed over heaters to dry.
- Check electrical appliances are turned off when they are not required e.g. wax heater.
- Never overload electrical circuits.
- Know where fire extinguishers are kept; which one to use; how to use it.

> **Practise evacuation procedure** – as follows:
> **If a fire starts: stop**
> **think**

Q: **Is it very small?**

A If yes, fetch the appropriate fire-fighting equipment and take action

Q: **Is it big? Too large to attempt fighting it yourself?**

A: If yes, then stay calm

- **raise** the alarm;
- **get your client**(s) to safety (outside);
- **leave the salon** quickly;
- **turn off** electrical appliances if possible;
- **close windows** if there is time;
- **close doors** as you leave;

- **ring the emergency services** (or delegate someone to do so), **dial 999** and give **your name**, **the address** and **details** of the fire.

REMEMBER

- **check your fire alarm regularly;**
- **have a fire drill periodically;**
- **check fire extinguishers are operative.**

Information can be obtained from your local (regional) fire department. Professional advice will be given in relation to your business.

MATERNITY RIGHTS

The Employment Act of 1980 and 1982 and the 1996 Social Security Act allows the expectant mother certain statutory rights:

- to take paid time off for ante-natal visits;
- to complain of unfair dismissal because of pregnancy;
- to return to work after a period of leave due to pregnancy or confinement;
- to receive maternity pay (subject to certain conditions).

The statutory maternity pay the employee receives is claimed back by the employer in the same way as sick pay. **Current information can be obtained from**: Inland Revenue, Employer's Quick Guide to PAYE and NICS, CWGI-1998 and DTI booklet, Maternity Rights – A Guide for Employers and Employees.

Statutory Maternity Pay abbreviations and terms

Expected Week of Confinement (EWC)	The week when the baby is due.
Qualifying Week (QW)	The fifteenth week before the EWC.
Maternity Pay Period (MPP)	The period of up to 18 weeks during which SMP can be paid.
	The MPP can start at any time between the 11th week before the EWC and the Sunday following the date the baby is born.
	The start of the MPP is affected if the employee is absent with a pregnancy related illness on or after the beginning of the 6th week before the EWC.

Who can get Statutory Maternity Pay ?.....

To get SMP an employee must:

- have been continuously employed by you for at least 26 weeks continuing into the QW
- still be pregnant at the 11th week before the week the baby is due or have had the baby by that time

- have average weekly earnings of not less than the lower earnings limit for the payment of NICs which applies on the Saturday of the QW. See the April 1998 supplement to CA29 for changes to calculating the average earnings
- have given you notice of the date her MPP is due to start at least 21 days beforehand

- have given you medical evidence of the date her baby is due/born within 3 weeks of the start of her MPP. In exceptional circumstances this can be extended to 13 weeks. See CA29 under 'Medical evidence'
- have stopped working for you

If an employee satisfies **all** six conditions, she qualifies for SMP even if she does not intend to work for you after her baby is born.

If an employee is not entitled to SMP, give her form SMP1 so that she can claim Maternity Allowance from the Benefits Agency. Form SMP1 can be obtained from the Contributions Agency via your local Social Security Office.

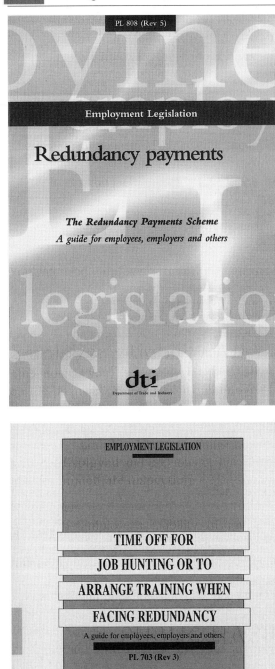

Figure 5.4 Redundancy and Maternity Rights Booklets

REDUNDANCY

An employee can become redundant when the **employer ceases to trade** or the **employer needs to reduce the workforce**.

Employers are required to pay a **redundancy payment** (a lump sum payment).

The amount varies according to:
- the age of the person and the length of continuous service;
- the employee must have worked for at least 16 hours a week and for a minimum of two years or 8 hours per week for a minimum of five years.

The employee is entitled to notice:
- one week if employed for under two years but more than a month;
- two weeks for over two years and an additional week for each year of employment (maximum 12 weeks).

An employee is also entitled to time off to look for a new job if employment has been continuous for 2 years full-time or 5 years part-time.

The **DTI** publishes **free booklets** which give detailed current information:
1. *Time Off For Job Hunting Or To Arrange Training When Facing Redundancy PL703 Rev3*
2. *Redundancy Consultation and Notification PL 833 (Rev4)*
3. *Redundancy Payments PL808 (Rev5)*

ACAS – ADVISORY CONCILIATION AND ARBITRATION SERVICE

ACAS is an independent organisation set-up under the Employment Protection Act 1975. ACAS offers services to you on matters that relate to employment or industrial relations, such as disputes and dismissals and will provide booklets on many aspects of employment. The main office in London is at:

Clifton House
83–117 Euston Road
London NW1 2RB
Public Enquiry Point is 020 7396 5100
ACAS Reader Ltd. 01455 852225

Self Assessments and Activities

1 According to the Health and Safety Act 1974, an employer must provide a safe place to work. List the responsibilities you would have:

   (a) to your staff; and

   (b) to your clients:

   if you were an employer.

2 Give the reasons for a salon to have an accident record book.

3 List the statutory rights of the expectant mother according to the Employment Acts of 1980 and 1982 and the Social Security Act 1996.

4 Employers are required to pay a redundancy payment. Comment on this as a salon owner.

5 Explain the importance of section 3 in the six pack (EU regulations 1992): 'The provision and use of work equipment regulations 1992'.

6 Describe the role of an Environmental Health Officer in relation to the running of a beauty salon.

7 Identify the purpose of a 'risk assessment'.

8 Name the act that has been put in place to ensure that the workplace is safe and healthy for employees and visitors.

9 Explain what you understand by the terms PPE and DSE.

10 Name the act that aims to control the use of electrical equipment.

11 Explain the term PAT testing.

12 Describe the particular concerns of the Working Time Regulations 1998.

13 Design a check sheet for the weekly monitoring of electrical equipment in the salon.

14 Explain

   (a) the fire precautions you would need to take in your salon

   (b) the type of fire-fighting equipment that would be necessary.

CHAPTER 6

Communication skills

<table>
<tr><td>

OBJECTIVES

This chapter explains the salon owner's role in establishing effective staff and client communications, the skills in handling objections and developing a good telephone manner, and the way to maintain a satisfied clientele.

</td></tr>
</table>

As a salon owner you are the person who is responsible for good staff relations. You are:

manager/counsellor

human resources/personnel

beauty therapist

You have several **major roles** to play and you may need to perfect certain skills and evaluate your own attitudes. **Good listening skills** and **understanding** are vital. A genuine interest in your staff as people and not only as employees is very important.

Communication can be **verbal**, **visual** or **non-verbal**. **Body language** often conveys a very different message to what is being said, and **eye movements** can also tell a person exactly what you are thinking. The **tone of voice** and the manner in which you speak and present yourself is all communicated to the receiver. Ask yourself:

> will *my* approach be easy and sincere
> or
> arrogant and dictatorial?

Once you have acquired the best skills your verbal communication will be easy. You must then consider how it will be most effective. (If you feel that you need further assistance in verbal communication there are a number of courses offered by Adult Education Centres. There are also tape cassette courses available from your local library.)

Any instructions should be:

clear

concise

Then they will be understood easily.

Often it is necessary to reinforce instructions, so they should also be written. A memo is ideal for this and you will have a copy of it. This will:

help to prevent a mistake

help the person not to forget

Memorandum

DATE: January 11, 2000

TO: [Names]

FROM: [Names]

RE: [Subject]

CC: [Names]

[Type your memo text here]

EFFECTIVE CLIENT LIAISON

Enquirers to your salon are potential clients. Therefore, it is important to ensure that your staff are trained continually in good client liaison. It is never wasted. The way your clients are received is most important.

Remember

first impressions count: always welcome your enquirer with your face and voice.

'Good morning'.

> Smile greeting

'My name is . . .'

> Identify yourself:

'Can I help you?'

> Offer service:

As the salon owner you know the importance of **visual communication and body language**. It is important that your face and body reflect what is being said. Your client will know whether you are sincere.

> The enquirer (unknown person)

is a valuable person – she will probably become a client.

 Remember
without clients there is *no* business.

If the enquirer wants information she will ask for it.

> Make sure information is:

accurate and detailed and answers her questions.

Keep it simple:

- speak to the enquirer in language that she understands;
- explain the treatments carefully; and
- make sure the enquirer is satisfied with your explanation.

If it is absolutely necessary for you to leave the enquirer, ensure that **you excuse yourself** with politeness and courtesy at **all** times.

Never leave the enquirer too long – return as soon as possible. When you have dealt with the enquirer's needs, check through them again. Does she want to make an appointment? If so, make the appointment. If she is uncertain, ensure she has the salon card and leaflets before she leaves.

Bid your enquirer **goodbye** with the same pleasant manner that you greeted her.

 Remember
she is a potential client.

TELEPHONE ENQUIRIES/CLIENT HANDLING

Telephone enquiries should receive the same courteous attention as your caller.

Never leave your enquirer unattended on the telephone.

Using effective interpersonal skills

The discerning client expects a lot from the beauty therapist.

There are often many salons for her to choose from so she can afford to be selective.

Initially the enquirer may make a telephone enquiry. How her call is dealt with will often determine whether she becomes a client.

What will she expect when she rings?
- a prompt reply
- a pleasant manner
- accurate knowledgeable information (length of treatment, cost . . .)
- an appointment

If **a receptionist is employed to answer telephone calls** (see interview pages 160–1) it is vital that she has a knowledge of the salon treatments. If she is unable to answer the enquirers' questions it is important that there is someone who can offer the expertise. This information needs to be given promptly. It is never good practice to keep a client waiting on the telephone. This creates the impression that the establishment is not properly managed. Telephone enquiries may be ringing to **change** or **cancel** their appointments.

Remember to do this immediately and to re-book them.

Mistakes occur in the appointment book because writing is not clear. Action it straight away and:
- save time;
- save embarrassment later;
- save a client.

Remember

- your enquirer cannot see you, she has only your voice as communication.
Ensure that your telephone service is:
- prompt;
- pleasant;

- professional;

and that your information is;

- accurate;
- relevant;
- understood.

When your enquirer becomes a client she deserves:

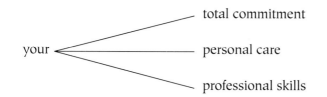

your — total commitment

— personal care

— professional skills

> **REMEMBER** effective client liaison is achieved by:
>
> - respect;
> - consideration;
> - skilled work;
> - a genuine interest in the client.

The therapist

You will need to:

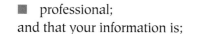

Listen

to her needs carefully and sensitively.

Needs

plan her treatments so that her needs are met and you have given the best advice.

Result

a satisfied client.

Consider your own problems before you start work – then, as a true professional, put them aside. The client does not come to the salon to hear extra problems – she will probably have enough of her own.

The client

Salon treatments offer your client:

- a temporary opportunity to escape from problems;
- the chance to be pampered;
- permission to unwind and relax.

Make sure your client can do this.

A satisfied client:

returns

|

speaks well of the salon

|

speaks well of you

|

recommends you/the salon

|

keeps *you* in business

CLIENT CONSULTATION

The **client consultation** is very important. Increasingly, we are aware of the significance of studying the whole person in order to be able to offer the **best advice** and ultimately the most appropriate treatments.

This means that sufficient times must be allowed for the **consultation** to be conducted. If it is the client's first appointment, this must be taken into account at the time of booking the appointment.

Sometimes a client will choose to come for a **consultation first** and book the treatment on a different day. This can be a good idea, as it can show contra-indications for a particular treatment.

The consultation

The consultation is your *key to successful business*. It serves several vital purposes:

- the opportunity to **meet, welcome** and get to know your client – to establish good communication and put your client at ease.
- to establish a good rapport and trust
- the chance to **listen** to the client's needs
- the ability to **establish the client's needs** and assess her suitability for treatment and to record relevant details
- the opportunity to **explain** the treatments available

- the opportunity to **demonstrate** your professional expertise by explaining treatments **in language that the client understands**
- the scope to design **a personal treatment plan** for the client and, on her agreement, to confirm the sale.

Points to note

Develop your communication skills:

- **listen** to your client;
- **talk** with your client;
- watch her body language;
- remember vital information;
- try not to write, head down, all the time you are recording information.

How you ask the question determines how the client answers.

Direct questions usually require short concise answers, e.g. **are you** taking any medication?

Open questions allow the client to explain more fully, e.g. **tell me** about your skin problem.

Clients may be **quiet, nervous, shy**. They **will** need encouragement to give the answers you need. Some clients are **assertive, dominant** and **direct** – they will need a calm, firm approach so that they know you are fully in control of the consultation.

As the consultation develops you will no doubt start to be aware of some of your client's needs. Sometimes the client has a particular problem which she will disclose on another visit, such as superfluous hair in a sensitive region.

Remember

- Always question carefully – there may be some very delicate areas that the client doesn't wish to discuss at this stage.

Sometimes clients do not give you the true facts – they tell you what they think you **ought** to know. To engage their trust takes time and expertise, and shows the importance of establishing a good rapport and confidence.

Try to record **all** the client's needs.

She may start by requesting facial treatments but consider body treatments for a later date.

All initial consultations require:

- personal details;
- medical history;
- lifetyle pattern;

- contra-indications;
- contra-actions;
- skin/figure analysis;
- treatment plan;
- skin sensitivity tests if applicable;
- client consent/signature;
- therapist's signature.

Follow up sessions require:
- checking of the above detail;
- a record of the treatment session and results;
- home care routine/suggestions;
- a written copy for your client.

Remember

Check your **insurance policy** for any additional **requirements** re:
- sun-tanning sessions;
- micro-pigmentation;
- electrical epilation;
- waxing;
- AHA peeling.

HANDLING OBJECTIONS

It is always important when handling objections to remember your attitude towards the situation and person.

Always

be sincere – put your opinion across ensuring that you are not using language which promotes aggression, for example, the use of the word 'you' in this situation is often over-emphasised and is therefore seen as aggressive.

Try

to reach a solution you are both satisfied to accept.

Remember
your tone of voice and your attitude are important.

Check your reactions

they can be:

aggressive: 'Have you?', and

passive: 'Well . . . I don't know.', or

assertive: 'What is the problem, can I help?'

We know that clients are *not* always right, though they would like us to believe that they are. In the beauty profession it is vital the client receives the treatment that is correct for her. Occasionally, clients want a treatment that is unsuitable. How will you advise your clients?

There are many ways of handling this, but first you must be convinced that the treatment is unsuitable:

 The sincerity of your approach is important because it is necessary that the client trusts your opinion.

 Your professional expertise.

You might start by **identifying** and **empathising** with the client: 'I can understand why you would like . . .' and then emphasise why the treatment is unsuitable and positively suggest an alternative.

Emphasise the **benefits** of the alternative treatment:

- how it will meet the client's **needs**; and
- its suitability.

Do not be too 'pushy'.

Keep a steady, even voice explaining the best treatment for her. If the client feels comfortable with your explanation and advice, she will either say or communicate her feelings non-verbally, for example nod her head.

Finally ask if you can go ahead. This method works only if you practise it well and genuinely believe that you are giving the client the **best advice**. The client will recognise this.

If you offer alternatives without a good reason, often you will lose a client because she will feel pressured into agreeing with you.

➡️ *Remember*

when handling an objection

empathise with the client
|
identify with the client
|
offer a solution
|
wait for the client's agreement

Assisting the therapist

As the salon owner you will need to give your staff:

➡️ ■ advice
■ training

on how to deal with complaints.

This can be difficult for new or inexperienced members of staff.

They must learn to deal with complaints as they occur in the salon. However, you or a senior person should always be available for support.

You may draw up a **code of practice** such as this:
■ always remain calm
■ take the client to a quiet area
■ offer her a seat
■ ask the client to explain the problem (complaint)
■ listen
■ show interest in your client and be understanding and diplomatic
■ if the client is being difficult you need supervisory assistance
■ if the client is being reasonable you may offer a solution
■ you will need to consult with the supervisor if you are offering a refund or alternative treatment.

Remember

■ stay calm;
■ never get angry;
■ there is always someone to help you.

Self Assessments and Activities

1 Draw a chart to show how good communication skills can achieve good results in the salon.

2 Show how you would answer a telephone enquiry. Create a role-play situation.

3 Write a short dialogue to show how you would handle an objection from a client regarding her choice of beauty treatment.

4 A good rapport is important when dealing with clients. List ten points that show how you would establish a good rapport with a client.

5 Select a treatment, design a treatment card and discuss how you would take a client through the consultation process.

6 Give examples of **direct questions** and **open questions** when conducting a client consultation. Explain when open questions are necessary and why direct questions can be a definite disadvantage.

7 Explain how you would deal with the following types of caller

   a)   an enquiry regarding job vacancies;

   b)   a dissatisfied client.

8 List 10 points that show how you would establish a good rapport with a client.

9 How would you improve communication skills in the salon between therapists?

10 Explain the information you should take when talking to an enquirer on the telephone.

11 Explain why is it necessary to know the costs and services offered in the salon.

12 Describe the importance of the receptionist.

13 Describe how you would deal with a client complaint.

14 Send a memo to your staff informing them that there are some retail products missing and that it will be necessary to check security procedures. Arrange a staff meeting.

Interview with Carol – lecturer/trainer and mobile therapist
Q: What type of course did you originally take?
I took a 3 year Hair and Beauty Therapy Course at Havering College, in 1983. It led to a City & Guilds qualification in Hairdressing and Wigmaking and Beauty Therapy and Epilation.

Q: What was your initial ambition?
I've never been that self-confident and initially I would have been happy to get a job in a salon.

Q: What made you go into teaching?
I'd had the experience of several salons behind me and had also managed a ladies health club in Westminster and was running my own mobile business and it was going really well. I had more clients than I could cope with but I missed the studying and needed some brain stimulation. So I signed up for the C&G FAETC part-time Teacher's Certificate.

Q: Please give a brief account of your career to date.
Well I got my first job in Pamela Steven's Beauty Clinic through my college's work experience scheme. The owner had a chain of salons, so I was able to work in Knightsbridge and Holloway Road in North London. From there I went to work in Health Haven, a ladies-only health club, where I was eventually promoted to Manageress of the treatment rooms.

I then set up a mobile practice and that did really well, but as my confidence grew I felt ready to cope with more responsibility and signed up for the Teaching Certificate at Kingston College. I managed to get 4 hours teaching a week and absolutely loved it! The Beauty Department was quite small in 1987 and the only full-time Lecturer who had basically been co-ordinating the courses decided to leave following the birth of her baby. I was encouraged to go for her job and didn't for one minute think that I would get it but I did!

From there my career really took off. I completed my Certificate in Education and became an assessor, and this meant that I was able to assess students working towards an NVQ and was offered the post of Curriculum Support Manager. This led to the eventual promotion to Head of Section in 1998.

During this time I also managed to have two wonderful children and it was whilst I was on maternity leave that Helena Rubenstein approached me to train their Consultants.

After moving to West Sussex I decided I needed to be more locally based and now find myself at Lewes Tertiary College where I have the grand title of Beauty Therapy Co-ordinator. I juggle this job with freelance work as a Trainer and Consultant for Helena Rubenstein and my mobile work fills in the gaps.

Q: Tell me more about your role at Helena Rubenstein.
Well I have been offered various types of work from giving quotes to Beauty Journalists, helping out with Press Releases to running Skin care Workshops around the country not to mention training their Consultants.

Q: How does a busy lecturer keep up their practical skills?
Well that's difficult especially with two children under 5 years old, but I run a small mobile practice and have invested in a range of portable equipment and treat my clients in the privacy of their own home.

Q: Tell me more about your job with Lewes Tertiary College.
Well I'm contracted to work 22.5 hours a week and basically my job role involves developing and implementing NVQ2 and NVQ3. I have recently achieved my D34 and this has given me extra responsibility in that I am qualified to sign off the students and claim their certificates. This means that I have to monitor all the staff and the courses they teach on.

Q: What are your immediate career plans?
At the moment my career is on hold until the children are in school full-time. However, I do enjoy the training side of things and I love organising and setting up initiatives. I am also looking forward to finishing a text book that I am writing at the moment.

Q: What qualities do you look for when selecting a lecturer for part-time work.
They should have at least 3–5 years of commercial experience for a start, they need to be friendly and approachable and hold or be working towards a teaching qualification and assessors award.

Q: How important is job satisfaction to you?
Really important, I can't tell you how proud I feel when I visit a salon for a treatment or on a work experience visit and the salon manageress or owner is an ex-student!

Q: Is there a down side to teaching?
You have to be really disciplined about marking students' work and preparing lessons through your holidays and most evenings, even after a hard day's work. You are setting an example to your students every day, so it is vital that you remain the professional role model. I must admit it's a struggle to juggle my commitments at the moment with my children being so young but I'm sure that it will get easier as they become older! And there's always room for improvement with my time management skills!

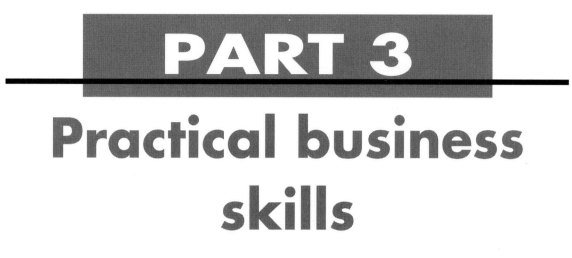

PART 3

Practical business skills

CHAPTER 7

Purchasing or renting your business

OBJECTIVES

This chapter looks at purchasing or renting a business; the location of the business and the specialist advice that you may need to seek; the type of property you might choose; and what you need to look for when you think you have found the 'right' premises.

You have made the decision to become your own boss:

- You can **buy** your salon in a town, the country, or at a resort.
- You can **rent** a salon in the above places or in an **hotel**.
- You can be a **mobile** beauty therapist.

LOCATION

If you buy your salon/business what must you consider?
- Where will it be?
- How will you decide?

The position of your salon can be the difference between success and failure.

Businesses are advertised in local or regional advertisers. This will show you what is available and give some idea of the prices. Then you will need to talk to a **commercial estate agent**.

The commercial estate agent will be able to offer information about the businesses that are 'for sale' with his company and also give general advice, for example, council application for a change of use, if you wish to change the nature of the existing business.

This is the time to carry out a SWOT analysis. This is a simple means of assessing the:

S	strengths
W	weaknesses
O	opportunities
T	threats

to business. You might consider the following in your analysis.

Check the area you have chosen. Are there any proposed development plans for:

new businesses?

housing?

You will probably consider an area you know well so that you are familiar with the local amenities. Does it have:

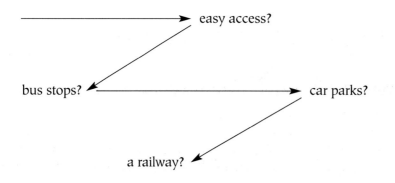

Is it:

■ near to other shops?
■ a successful area?

If you are starting from scratch, you must be sure there is a market for beauty therapy. You may need to consider some *market research*.

If buying an existing salon, you will want to check carefully the salon's financial history. Is the trade increasing or decreasing? You will want to check with local authorities and the environmental requirements.

> ***NOTE!*** Careful checking and groundwork can save making a mistake.

TYPE OF PREMISES

What type of premises will you buy:

| *freehold* | or | *leasehold* |

| | | | |

this means you
will *own*
the property

this means you will lease/rent
a property for an agreed period
|
it is legally binding?
|
often has restrictions
|
you could be responsible for repairs
and maintenance
|
rents can be reviewed
|
various other considerations
may apply

PROFESSIONAL ADVISORS

When buying a business you will need:

■ A **surveyor** to be sure you know the value of the property. A full structural survey tells you about most aspects of the property, including plumbing and electricity.

Valuations are a necessary expense. You can save yourself a lot of money by obtaining accurate information from them. You can also be advised about fire requirements which may not have been updated in the property. This is information of vital importance.

■ An **accountant** to advise you on the **vendor's** (the person selling) accounts, and financing your business.

■ A **solicitor** to advise on the legal terms of a contract and to transact the business contract, when you decide to buy.

When you find the business you intend to purchase, you will want to examine the accounts of the vendor to evaluate the business and the price that is being asked. The accounts will show what expenditure has to be made and what income there has been. They will show:

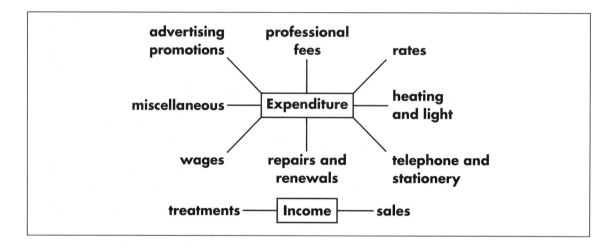

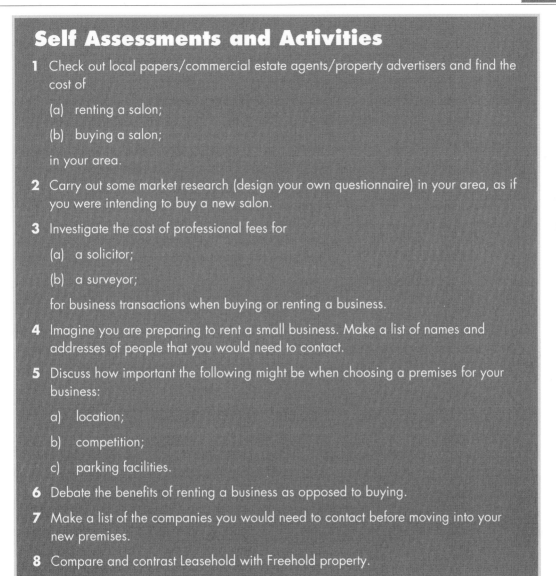

Self Assessments and Activities

1 Check out local papers/commercial estate agents/property advertisers and find the cost of

(a) renting a salon;

(b) buying a salon;

in your area.

2 Carry out some market research (design your own questionnaire) in your area, as if you were intending to buy a new salon.

3 Investigate the cost of professional fees for

(a) a solicitor;

(b) a surveyor;

for business transactions when buying or renting a business.

4 Imagine you are preparing to rent a small business. Make a list of names and addresses of people that you would need to contact.

5 Discuss how important the following might be when choosing a premises for your business:

a) location;

b) competition;

c) parking facilities.

6 Debate the benefits of renting a business as opposed to buying.

7 Make a list of the companies you would need to contact before moving into your new premises.

8 Compare and contrast Leasehold with Freehold property.

CHAPTER 8

Key Skills
C
AN
IT
IOLP
WWO

How to finance your business

OBJECTIVES

This chapter deals with financing your business and the various options that you may consider to raise capital. It explains the importance of a business plan and the need to have some personal security. The value of partnerships, limited partnerships, limited companies, and sole trading and franchising are considered.

Once you have decided to buy your own business you will need to consider **finance**. If you have personal savings to invest this could be a good start, but where will the balance come from?:

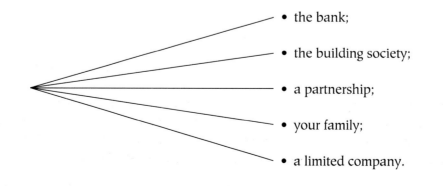

- the bank;

- the building society;

- a partnership;

- your family;

- a limited company.

Your accountant will advise how much you will need to borrow, then you need to look at your options.

THE BANK

Any of the major banks will expect you to prepare a **detailed business plan** so that they can see if your venture is worthwhile. The plan should show full details about:

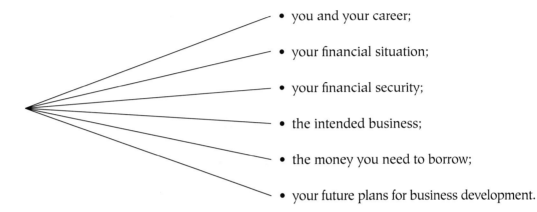

- you and your career;
- your financial situation;
- your financial security;
- the intended business;
- the money you need to borrow;
- your future plans for business development.

Banks can offer more than just a loan or a mortgage. They offer financial advice and services which are of benefit to the business owner. Some banks offer their own package and business start-up guide, which give ideas, advice and guidelines to setting up and operating a small business. It includes preparing your business plan. Check with *all* the banks to see what is on offer.

The bank may offer you a commercial mortgage or a loan. A **mortgage** is usually a long-term loan with regular monthly payments, including interest; a **loan** can be short- or long-term with regular monthly payments, including interest. A bank will usually expect you to offer some security for a loan so that it knows its money is safe. It will also expect you to invest an equal amount into the business or property.

➡ *Remember*

the business plan is very important.

Most banks have produced packages to assist the Small Business. The *NatWest* **Start-up Planner and Guide 'Book'** gives very detailed information for the would be business person. This includes a sample Business Plan and how to operate a Budget. It includes a disk for use on a PC, which will help you to create your Business Plan and Operating Budget. This information is **free**. There is additional banking service, **Business Manager** (free for 2 months) which could assist you in operating your business accounts once you have become established.

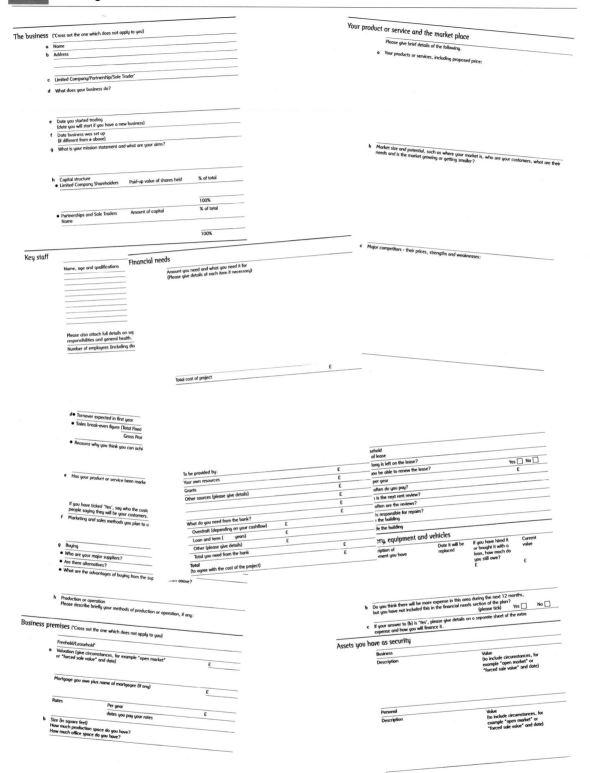

Figure 8.1 NatWest's Business Plan

THE BUILDING SOCIETY

The building society can offer mortgages on business property but this is not an easy option to pursue. It is necessary to contact individual building societies to see what facilities are available.

PARTNERSHIPS

This can be very useful when establishing a business if one person or several people (up to 20) wish to invest.

Points to consider:
- each partner is responsible for the other's debts;
- each partner shares the profits;
- individual goals and ideas may vary;
- you need to know the person(s) very well.

If a partnership is formed, it is not absolutely necessary to have a written agreement, but it is strongly advisable. Your solicitor will advise you and prepare the agreement.

Limited partnerships

This type of partnership protects the individual in the agreement. A partner(s) is only responsible for debts to the total that she has put into the business – but one partner must accept unlimited liability. The limited partner has no management powers, but she does share the profits and does have a right to see the accounts. A limited partnership must be registered with the Registrar of Companies.

THE FAMILY

Someone in your family may wish to assist in financing your business, either in a private capacity or in a partnership. The arrangements would be made between the two of you and probably an agreement drawn up by your solicitor.

A LIMITED COMPANY

This could be set up when you have established your business. A limited company is when two or more persons want to own the company. They are the **shareholders**. A limited company may be **private** or **public (plc)**.

A **private company** does not offer shares to the public. A **plc** offers shares to the public. A limited company must be registered by the Registrar of Companies. For more information and registration forms contact:

(England and Wales)
Companies House
Crown Way
Maindy
Cardiff CF4 3UZ

(Scotland)
Companies Registration Office
100–102 George Street
Edinburgh EH2 3DJ

(Northern Ireland)
Companies Registry
IDB House
64 Chichester Street
Belfast BT 4JX

FRANCHISING

This is not really a way of financing your business, it is an alternative business proposition. Franchising is when a *patent organisation*, the **franchisor**, establishes a format for operating a business. The franchisor establishes:

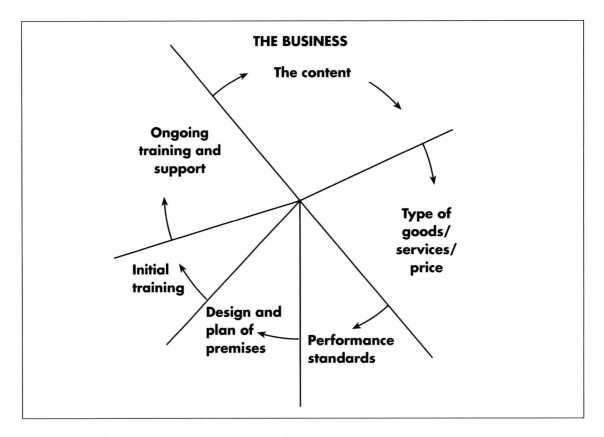

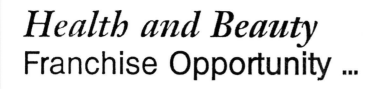

Health and Beauty
Franchise Opportunity ...

Coming in Cambridge in June 1999, this is the first in a series of health & fitness developments by The Greenalls Group plc.

The result of extensive market research, 'Greens Health & Fitness' will comprise 40,000 square feet of the highest quality aerobics, swimming, spa, beauty and bistro facilities. Moreover, it will be highly innovative and individualistic, quite unlike anything currently on the market.

Our health and beauty suite will be managed by a franchisee. It will have its own reception area and 5 beauty therapy rooms, equipped to the highest of standards. In addition, as the franchisee, you will be given encouragement and space to develop your business by marketing to both Greens club members and non-members. Greens priority is to ensure a consistently high quallity of beauty service. The franchisee will be required to pay a monthly rental.

This is a unique opportunity for an experienced Beauty Professional who can demonstrate sound business acumen allied to commercial experience. If you think you have what we are looking for in Cambridge, or possibly elsewhere in the future, please write to the following address enclosing full details. A short list of applicants will be sent further information and invited to tender for an initial 12-month franchise term.

PLEASE WRITE TO: ANGELA LEWIS, SECRETARY TO OPERATIONS DIRECTOR, GREENS HEALTH AND FITNESS, PO BOX 333, THE MALT BUILDING, GREENALLS AVENUE, WARRINGTON, CHESHIRE WA4 6HL

Figure 8.2 Advertisement for a franchise

The franchisor then 'sells' the package (the franchise) to a business person (the franchisee). The franchisee pays an initial fee and a percentage of his profits. There is:

professional management expertise of a
business system
|
training and on-going support
|
the complete package for the salon
|
advertising
|
restricted freedom in the business
|
percentage payments to the franchisor
can be costly.

If you consider a franchise always discuss all aspects of it with your solicitor and make sure your Franchise Company has a good track record and is a member of the British Franchise Association.

So there are several options open to you. If you decide to go it alone with no partner, you will become a **sole trader**.

Sole traders are entirely responsible for all **debts** of the business as well as having all the **profits**. This means that should you get into financial difficulty your personal possessions could be at risk.

There are many ways in which you can obtain free advice:

■ **government schemes** have been set up to help small businesses;

Training and Enterprise Councils (TECS): these are independent local companies led by local business people, working under performance related contracts to the government. They must encourage economic growth through effective training and enterprise;

■ **local enterprise agencies and the DTI's** (Department of Trade and Industry) Enterprise Initiative;

All offer current information and advice for new businesses.

Self Assessments and Activities

Obtain a 'property advertiser' and find:

1 A business for sale – imagine you intend to purchase or rent it. Itemise the procedure you would use.

2 Draw up a business plan that you could present to a bank in order to obtain a loan.

3 There are advantages and disadvantages to a partnership. Imagine you are considering this and make a list of the pros and cons.

4 You need to raise £10,000 for setting-up your salon. Consider where you might go to raise the finance, how much interest you will pay, and for how long you will have the loan.

5 List the professional fees that you would need to take into account when purchasing premises.

6 Prepare a 'business plan' using the guidance in this chapter together with information from your local bank.

7 Compare and contrast Mobile Therapy with a High Street Salon.

8 Find out about one company that offers beauty franchises. Compare the advantages and disadvantages of being a franchisee.

9 You need an additional £15 000 to start up a small business renting space in a busy hair salon, in sub-groups decide where you might go to raise this finance.

CHAPTER 9

Key Skills
IOL

Business insurance

OBJECTIVES

This chapter deals with business insurance for buildings, contents, employer's liability, public liability and product liability. Professional indemnity and insurance claims – The Facts. The Woolf Report 1999.

BUILDINGS AND CONTENTS INSURANCE

Your business will need to be *insured* whether you own or rent it. If you own the business, you are responsible for:

insuring ——————— the building
    \——————— the contents

Insure the **building** against:

fire
|
explosion
|
flood/storm
|
burglary
|
damage
/   \
accidental   malicious

Insure the **contents**:

fixtures
|
fittings
|
stock

These all must be insured against the same perils as the buildings.

Insure the **people**:

staff
|
customers

You will need **employer's liability insurance** and **public liability insurance**.

EMPLOYER'S LIABILITY INSURANCE

Employer's Liability Act 1969

This protects you, the employer, against any claims brought by an employee who may get injured on the premises. You must have **employer's liability insurance and the certificate must be displayed in the salon**.

Recent changes in **Employment Law** stipulate that the **Certificate of Employer's Liability Insurance** must now be kept for **40 years**. The **current certificates must still be displayed** and previous certificates should be kept in 'accessible storage' and be available for **immediate inspection**.

Remember

Employer's Liability Insurance is a statutory requirement and the definition of 'employee' is very wide. It includes voluntary helpers, work experience students, hired or contract workers and several other categories.

If an employee is injured through her own negligence, this is not covered.

PUBLIC LIABILITY INSURANCE

This protects you in case a member of the public is injured on your premises. **Public Liability Insurance** is not compulsory but it is **advisable**. This protects you, the employer, if a member of the public is injured or has personal property damaged by you or another employee. A claim for compensation can be very expensive if professional negligence is proved. This type of insurance cover will provide you with the cost of legal fees as well as compensation.

PROFESSIONAL INDEMNITY INSURANCE

This can be included in your Public Liability Insurance Policy. This insurance covers **named** employees against claims by clients, where personal injury or damage has resulted directly from a treatment.

Individual professional beauty therapists **should have this insurance protection**. This can be obtained through the various professional associations in beauty and therapy. It is not compulsory.

PRODUCT LIABILITY INSURANCE

This is also a very essential part of your insurance. Make certain it is included in your policy. It will protect you against claims arising from products which are not necessarily the manufacturer's responsibility and which may be your responsibility. If a product is being used in a claim as unsuitable there are many aspects that have to be checked and every person involved with the product can be held responsible. Product liability insurance helps to alleviate this by protecting the retailer/therapist.

A recognised broker (who will belong to the **British Association of Insurers**) will advise you on the type of insurance that is appropriate to your business. A broker will also 'shop around' to find you the best policy.

Alternatively, you can contact an insurance company directly and it will send a commercial insurance consultant to advise you and give a quotation most suited to your business. You will pay a **premium** for your insurance protection, either annually or monthly by cheque or direct debit.

Insurance premiums are high, but are a necessity and can protect:

yourself

|

your business

|

your staff

|

your clients

|

your future

NOTE! Never economise on insurance

Make sure that:

your policy is index-linked
(rises per annum according to the level of inflation)

|

you have a 'new for old' policy
(this covers the replacement cost of your articles)

|

your policy suits your requirements

INSURANCE CLAIMS

Insurance claims in the Beauty Industry have been steadily increasing. You will need to ensure that you have the cover you need and that you understand the policy, and in particular any exclusions or special conditions. Know the action you should take if any incident occurs that might give rise to a claim being made.

In **April 1999 The Woolf Report** introduced certain changes to provide a 'fast track' system for Personal Injury claims to the value of £15,000. (These changes only affect English Law.)

Insurance Policies affected by the changes are:
- Employers Liability;
- Public Liability (including Treatment Risks) policies;
- Product Liability;
- Motor Third Party Liability.

The pre-action protocol required is:
- a claimant must notify **you** in writing, before any legal action is taken, of their intention to claim. The notification must give **you** sufficient information to identify the alleged incident that gave arise to the claim.
- A written reply must be sent within 21 days of date of posting of letter of claim. Insurance details must be disclosed.
- Within 90 days of the letter of acknowledgement of claim, liability must either be accepted or declined.
- If the claim is declined, any documentation relied upon in support of it must be disclosed.

This means that as salon owner you must:
- report claims to your insurers immediately – 21 day deadline;
- give insurers all relevant documentation;
- provide insurers with full information as soon as possible – 90 day deadline;
- make sure your employees know their obligations with regard to reporting immediately any incident that might give rise to a claim by a client or an employee.

Did you know that:

- proper recorded and filed records are the basis of the insurers information to settle or challenge claims;
- often complaints arise as a result of clients ignoring aftercare instruction;
- clear records, demonstrating professional practice and clear advice/instructions are the best defence against fraudulent claims;
- it helps to establish evidence of good professional practice if printed after care instructions for some treatments (e.g. electrolysis and waxing) are given to individual clients. Such instructions should be 'gone through' verbally with the client before she departs;
- for some treatments insurers issue specific instructions requiring clients to sign at each treatment, that they have read the instructions/warnings e.g. sun-beds, toning tables, micro-pigmentation;
- some treatments carry 'special conditions' and client records should show that these have been observed. If not the insurers ability to 'take on' a claim is compromised and more importantly could invalidate the therapists cover;
- claims may arise months or sometimes years after the treatment and records of the original treatment should be available. e.g. micro-pigmentation, sun-tanning;
- insurance companies may require client records to be kept for 6 years and clients for sun-tanning should sign a warning notice on each and every occasion;
- all 'incidents' and subsequent events e.g. conversations, should be recorded in addition to normal client records and passed to the insurers should a claim be made;
- insurers always advise that any significant incident that might give rise to a claim should be reported to them at once.   **Source IPTI – 9/99**

Self Assessments and Activities

1 What types of insurance would you need to purchase to cover the following:
   a) yourself;
   b) your premises;
   c) a company car;
   d) salon stock;
   e) your clients.

2 Comment on the following types of insurance: Professional Indemnity Insurance, Public Liability Insurance and Employer's Liability Insurance.

3 State how long an Employer's Liability Insurance **Certificate** must be kept.

4 Obtain information from a commercial insurance company on
   a) the **type** of insurance package required for a small business;
   b) the **annual** premium.

5 List the key points to remember if a client is going to make an insurance claim against you.

CHAPTER 10

Key Skills
C
IT
PS
IOLP

Information Technology and your business

OBJECTIVES

This chapter tells you about the electronic systems that you might have in business, including a telephone, fax and a computer and the services that they can offer. You will need to consider the cost and benefits of using the electronic services, you must also be familiar with the Data Protection Act 1984 if you use a computer to store clients personal details.

There are a number of electronic systems that will assist you in business. Naturally you will want a **telephone**. It would be difficult to do business without one. With your 'phone you will need **voice mail** (answer phone) so that you can be sure not to miss out on any future business even when the salon is closed. It is important to return your caller's telephone call as quickly as possible so that you can be sure of your client's custom.

Facsimile transmission service (fax) can often be purchased with your telephone and is often cheaper than buying one separately. A fax machine transmits black and white documents or photos by using a telephone line to send it to your receiver's fax machine. You place your copy in the machine and it is reproduced for your receiver.

The advantages of this method are:
- it is quicker than the post;
- you can send it overseas;
- urgent matters can be dealt with immediately;
- it costs the same as a telephone call.

A computer

If you decide that your business would benefit from a computer you must first have IT skills or you must find a course where you can learn them. Evening classes offer a variety of courses for the beginner or/and business person.

When buying you computer you will also need the appropriate 'software' (packages) to suit your needs e.g. word-processing, accounts and database.

How could you benefit from a computer system as a salon owner?

You could:
- store client records, treatments, purchases (see Data Protection Act page 94);
- have a database for suppliers (electronic filing system);
- store salon records;
- stocktake;
- produce standard letters/letterheads and logos;
- produce price lists;
- leaflets for personalised mailshots (see page 168) – you will already have your clients names and addresses on your computer;
- create promotional material for advertising;
- keep a diary of appointments;
- keep staff records;
- keep your salon accounts and financial forecasting;
- your personal details.

You could also benefit from using **The Internet**.

The Internet is a world-wide collection of information submitted by companies, governments and private persons that you can access when you use the Internet.

To use the Internet you would need to belong to a 'Service Provider' such as: British Telecom (BT), Net Direct, AOL, Freeserve, Virgin etc.

Some Service Providers are free but others charge, depending on the service you require.

The Internet can provide current information on a vast range of subjects which may assist you and your business.

Electronic Mail – E-mail

E-mail is an Internet service, although there are still some Service Providers that offer e-mail connections only.

E-mail means that you can type a message into the computer and it is sent immediately to the person (who must also be on e-mail) by telecommunication. This message is stored with the other person's Service Provider until they access (go online) their Service Provider's system. The cost is the same as the telephone. It will depend on how much you use it!

Web Site

This is a collection of electronic documents. A web-page is a single document.

The World Wide Web

The World Wide Web is a collection of Web Sites which is available on the **Internet** in the form of documented information. These documents can be graphic or text published on the Internet by clickable hypertext links. By selecting the appropriate hypertext link the different information resources can be gathered from the World Wide Web. This is a very comprehensive way of calling up information.

DATA PROTECTION ACT 1984

You may use your computer to store personal details about your clients. If so, you may be required to register with the **Data Protection Registrar**, which means your business is placed on a public register of data users. You are required to comply with a code of practice for information handling **you must**:

- state what information is stored;
- how it will be used;
- the source of the information;
- to whom the information will be disclosed.

You are also required:

- to keep the information secure
- to keep the information accurate and relevant to your needs as detailed on the public register
- to reply to requests from individuals for any information you are holding on them.

Full details and registration forms are available from:

Data Protection Registrar
Wycliffe House
Water Lane
Wilmslow
Cheshire SK9 5AX
Tel: 01625 535777

Self Assessments and Activities

1 Prepare an appropriate message for your 'Voice Mail' in a busy salon.

2 Give two examples of when you might need to use a fax machine.

3 Find out about one website and one CD-ROM that is beauty related. Explain their benefits.

4 Using an IT resource centre at your college, design the following: A promotional leaflet for a popular treatment, A treatment plan for a facial client, your CV.

5 Obtain details of the Data Protection Act and explain how it affects the salon owner who stores personal details about clients on the computer.

CHAPTER 11

Keeping business records

OBJECTIVES

This chapter explains the details of keeping business records, whether you manage your own accounts or have an accountant. It deals with your day-to-day expenditure and income, and the necessary records you must keep for yourself and the Inland Revenue. More advanced bookkeeping and an accountant will be required as your business develops and you will need to forecast your cash flow.

Your accountant can produce a profit and loss account and a balance sheet, and will submit your accounts to the Inland Revenue. You will register for VAT if your business reaches an annual turnover of a certain limit. (You will need to check with your VAT office as this amount can change annually.)

Unless you are qualified in business accounting, it is always advisable to let your accountant advise you on procedure. Ultimately she will prepare your accounts to send to the Inland Revenue as you will have to pay tax on your profits.

Your accountant can show you how to record the daily business. There are many accounting book systems available, and it may be that your accountant will prefer you to use one of these. There are also a variety of computer packages for bookkeeping. By keeping accurate records you will be able to monitor the business and its development.

BANK ACCOUNTS

A cheque account will provide for your regular payments. A deposit account will enable you to save money for your income tax and accountant's fees. With your new accounts will come a detailed business guide for the small business (see page 81).

Check out what's on offer to you. In addition to Business Start-up Loans a bank may offer.

- free banking for a year;
- free book-keeping software package;
- free start-up guide;
- free 'business line' – 24 hour telephone banking service;
- free 'Help for your Business';
- a personalised information directory giving details of grants, training, local events that may help your business.

EXPENDITURE AND INCOME

You will need to keep details of your:

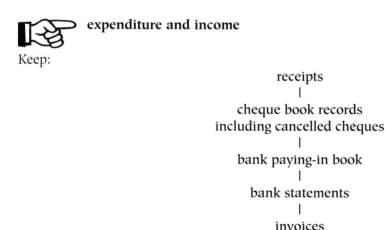 **expenditure and income**

Keep:

receipts
|
cheque book records
including cancelled cheques
|
bank paying-in book
|
bank statements
|
invoices

Expenditure such as:

rates
|
rent (if applicable)
|
heat
|
energy
|
insurance

postage/telephone/stationery
|
advertising
|
product
|
consumables
|
travel expenses
|
wages
|
bank charges

accountant's fees
|
salon expenses, for example, towels/gowns
|
staff training

CASH BOOKS

You will be able to start simple accounts and will need to keep a **cash book**. A simple way to record the day's takings would be to use a **sales receipt book**, either a duplicate book – or a book with a stub (so you have a copy). VAT is calculated at 17.5% at present.

For example:

Sales receipt	Sales receipt
I hour	I hour
b/massage	body massage
£23.50	£23.50
Date: 21.06.00	Date: 21.06.00
No. 200	No. 200 VAT included

Figure 11.1 Sample sales receipt

A simple **income cash book** could be drawn up like this:

Date	Sales receipt number	Detail		Amount	Output VAT
		Product	Service		
21.6.00	200		Body massage	£20.00	£3.50

Figure 11.2 Sample income cash book

An **expenditure cash book** like this:

Date	Invoice No.	Cheque No.	Details	Total Amount excl. VAT	Input VAT
21.6.00	TF 12650	0061252	Couch	£200.00	£35.00
21.6.00	Petty Cash	0061253	Postage	£4.00	–

Figure 11.3 Sample expenditure cash book

You may want to make this system more detailed by adding further columns after the VAT. These would be 'analysis' columns so that you can see easily the different areas of expenditure of income. For example:

Input VAT	Stationery	Postage	Heating	Product
				(and so on …

Figure 11.4 Sample expenditure analysis columns

Output VAT	Massage	Type of Services		
		Facial	Waxing	Manicure

Figure 11.5 Sample income cash analysis columns

This analysis is a good guide to how your business is progressing. It shows the popular services and products and the areas you need to consider for promotion. At the end of each week or month you can add up your income and expenditure. You can check all this information against your bank statement

You will also need a **petty cash book**. This shows your expenses for everyday small items, for example, postage. You should keep your petty cash records in the same way as your expenditure cash book. The petty cash money you will draw by cheque and show in the expenditure cash book.

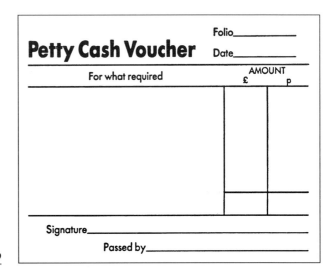

Figure 11.6 Petty cash slip

Bank reconciliation The only differences are usually payments or income that may not have gone through your bank account at the time of the statement, but they will show on your records.

When you have balanced your books, you will compare your findings with your **cash flow forecast** for the month. If there is a large difference in your calculations you will need to analyse the figures carefully in order to reduce expenditure.

CASH FLOW FORECAST

This considers the changes that will take place with the cash available in your business – the balance of money in your bank account. The dates that invoices are paid can affect your cash flow at the bank. If you consider your income and expenditure in advance, you are able to see the times when your cash flow is low and you can **plan ahead**:

 You may

reduce purchases during these months

arrange an overdraft for this period

The cash flow forecast helps you to prepare monthly in order to maintain your business.

Business Name:

Cashflow Forecast

Enter month — Figures rounded to £'s

		Budget	Actual	Budget	Actual	Budget	Actual	Budget	Actual	Budget	Actual	Budget	Actual	Budget	Actual	Budget	Actual	Budget	Actual	Budget	Actual	Budget	Actual	Total Budget	Total Actual
	Receipts																								
1	Sales (including VAT) - Cash																								
2	- Debtors																								
3	Other trading income																								
4	Loans you have received																								
5	New capital																								
6	Selling of assets																								
7	Other receipts																								
a	Total receipts																								
	Payments																								
8	Cash for goods you have bought																								
9	Payments to creditors																								
10	Owner or directors' withdrawals																								
11	Wages and Salaries (net)																								
12	PAYE/NI																								
13	Capital items (for example equipment and vehicles)																								
14	Transport and packaging																								
15	Rent or rates																								
16	Services																								
17	Loan repayments																								
18	Hire or leasing repayments																								
19	Interest																								
20	Bank or finance charges																								
21	Professional fees																								
22	Advertising																								
23	Insurance																								
24																									
25																									
26	VAT																								
27	Corporation tax and so on																								
28	Dividends																								
b	Total payments																								
c	Net cashflow (a-b)																								
29	Opening bank balance																								
d	Closing bank balance (c ± Line 29)																								

Basic assumptions - please give details of the assumptions you use when you fill in this form and list any other relevant ones on the next page.

Credit taken - the average time your creditors give you to pay.   Days

Credit given - the average time you give your debtors to pay.   Days

Figure 11.7 A cash flow forecast

BOOKKEEPING

As a business progresses, a more **advanced method** of calculating income will be necessary. You are able to purchase a **complete bookkeeping package** if you own a computer. There are several types of these on the market, but it would be advisable to check with your accountant before buying one to ensure the package suits your needs.

If you decide to keep records manually or employ a bookkeeper, you will need to be familiar with various stages of bookkeeping. You will need to keep a **sales day book**. This shows an individual record for each class of business or business customers.

A **purchases day book** shows an individual record of money/invoices you owe to business suppliers. The information from these **day books** is transferred to **ledgers**.

The ledger

This is a system which uses double entry bookkeeping. Sales are recorded on the left-hand side of a page and payments received on the right-hand side. It demands good bookkeeping skills and is best recorded by a professional.

Sales ledger

This has all the information from the sales day book.

Purchases ledger

This has all the information from the purchases day book.

A general (nominal) ledger

This brings both ledgers together and is divided into sections such as:

- debtors;
- creditors;
- bank balance;
- sales.

From this information your accountant can calculate various information. She can **forecast profit and loss**. This is how your business will achieve:

- the **sales** it will make;
- the **costs** it will have;
- the **profit** it will receive.

Your accountant can produce a **trial balance**. That is a list of debit and credit balances from the Ledger.

Your accountant can produce a **profit and loss account**. This shows the profit or loss made by a business over a set period of time.

She can produce a **balance sheet**. This gives an accurate total financial position of the business on a set date. The balance sheet shows:

current assets
(what the business owns: money, money owed);

current liabilities
(what the business owes: overdraft, suppliers).

PROFIT AND LOSS

Trading and Profit and Loss Account for the Period 1 May 1999–00

Sales   £   £

Purchases ⟶

Opening stock ⟶

Less Closing stock ⟶

This balance is taken from the **Sales** and leaves the **Gross profit**

Gross profit ⟶

(Rent) and rates ⟶

Light and heat ⟶

Wages ⟶

Telephone ⟶

Postage/stationery ⟶

Advertising ⟶

Travel expenses ⟶

Bank charges ⟶

This total is taken from the **Gross profit** and leaves the **Net profit**

Accountancy fees ⟶

Depreciation ⟶

Net profit

Figure 11.8 Sample trading and profit and loss account

Figure 11.8 shows that the profit and loss follows on from the trading account. First you have the:

gross profit

|

deduct trading expenses

|

leaves the net profit

Profit-budget form

	Month:		Month:		Month:		Month:		Month:		Month:		Totals:	
	Budget	Actual	Budget	Actual	Budget	Actual	Budget	Actual	Budget	Actual	Budget	Actual	Budget	Actual
Sales														
Less: materials														
wages														
Gross profit														
Overheads: salaries														
Rent, rates, water														
Insurance														
Repairs, renewals														
Heat, light, power														
Postage														
Printing, stationery														
Transport														
Telephone														
Professional fees														
Depreciation														
Interest charges														
Other														
Total overheads														
Trading Profit														

Figure 11.9 A computer spreadsheet

THE BALANCE SHEET

Finally your accountant will draw up the **balance sheet**. Your balance sheet is made up of several parts:

> Fixed assets

are items necessary for the business to function, that is, fixtures/fittings, equipment, motor vehicle

> Current assets

are stock that you hold – money in the bank, cash in hand

> Current liabilities

are short-term debts, interest on loans, overdrafts, unpaid bills.

The figure for net current assets is reached by taking your current liabilities from your current assets. The net current assets is then added to your fixed assets to give your total assets. The trading account shows the gross profit for the same period.

How will your accountant calculate this information?

At the end of your financial year when the accountant draws up the trading profit and loss account, she will:

total your sales

|

put your opening stock
(beginning of year) with
your purchases, then

|

deduct stock left over at
end of year (closing stock)

SCHEDULE D TAX

When your accounts are submitted to the Inland Revenue the profits of your business, as a sole-trader, are liable for income tax. This Schedule D tax is payable on the profits. You will pay this tax half yearly.

These depreciate in value each year and an allowance is made for this in the profit and loss account and it is shown on the balance sheet.

These are deducted from the above to give the **net current assets.**

These are added to your **fixed assets** to give your **total assets**

This is the **opening financial position**
The profit from the profit and loss account is then added

'Drawings': this is the money you personally draw from the business, depending on your trading situation, for example, sole-trader.

Balance sheet

Fixed assets	Cost	Depreciation	Balance
FIxtures/fittings equipment			

Current assets

Stock

Debtors

Cash in hand

Less *Current liabilities*

Creditors

Bank overdraft

(add to)

Net current assets

Total assets

Represented by

Capital

Opening capital

(add) Profit for year

Less drawings

Figure 11.10 Sample balance sheet

VAT (VALUE ADDED TAX)

This is a tax on goods and services. You have to register for VAT if your annual turnover (annual sales) is liable to exceed a certain limit. This level can change annually, so you will need to check with your VAT office. The present percentage of VAT is 17.5% and this is added to
  - products;
  - services.

Some products are exempt, for example, food and books.

If you pay VAT:

you will register with the **Customs and Excise Office**;

 you will send monthly or quarterly VAT payments (**returns**).

How VAT works

■ it is charged on your products and services (**output tax**); and

■ it is paid on your purchases (stock and equipment) – (**input tax**).

When sending your VAT return to the Customs and Excise, you will subtract the **input tax** from the **output tax** and the balance only is sent. If the **input tax** is higher than the **output tax** you may claim this back.

> **NOTE!** VAT records must be kept carefully and accurately.

VAT return

The VAT return is issued by the Customs and Excise. The main columns are input VAT and output VAT. The VAT return:

■ summarises the totals of input and output VAT;

■ arrives at a balance that will either be for the Customs and Excise or the salon owner.

If payment is due to the Customs and Excise, this must be paid promptly and by a set date after the end of the tax period, if not penalties and interest are charged.

Customs and Excise requires:

 accounts to be kept and these must be available when a VAT officer calls to examine them. Regular checks are made.

Your local VAT office will advise you of the procedure for VAT registration, or where to apply for registration. General details can be obtained from:

Customs and Excise
New Kings Beam House
22 Upper Ground
London SE1 9PS

Self Assessments and Activities

1 You will need a business account. Find out the differences between a business account and a private bank account.

2 Check out two packages and business guides offered by two high street banks.

3 Create a page in your daily income cash book showing 5 treatments (services) completed at a salon in a day and their cost. Calculate the output VAT.

4 Create a page in a daily petty cash book showing expenditure for five items.

5 Explain briefly the following in relation to book-keeping:

   (a) cash flow forecast;

   (b) a sales ledger;

   (c) a purchase ledger;

   (d) balance sheet;

   (e) opening financial position;

   (f) gross profit.

6 Explain the purpose of the VAT return.

7 Calculate the VAT on an invoice costing £255.

8 Explain what you understand by **petty cash**.

CHAPTER 12

Key Skills
C
AN
PS
IOLP

Keeping business records – employing staff

OBJECTIVES

This section deals with the financial responsibilities you have when employing staff. The Inland Revenue requires you to issue a pay advice slip and make deductions of income tax and National Insurance (NI). This information is recorded in a wages book.

A P.45 form must be issued when an employee leaves. There are four classes of NI contributions and this can be paid to the Department of Social Security weekly or monthly. Statutory Sick Pay must also be paid if the employee has been sick for four or more consecutive days.

You and your staff may consider a personal pension plan. This qualifies for tax relief and allows you to plan for your future.

The Stakeholder Pension (commences 2001) means that all employers must offer a pension scheme.

WHERE TO GET ADVICE

When you start in business, there are always places that you can obtain information. Your local tax office publishes a booklet 'Starting in Business'. This offers basic advice and helpful guidelines. The Inland Revenue and the Contributions Agency also publishes cards called the 'Employer's Quick Guide to . . .'. These may be useful to obtain when you want to employ staff. They advise you about deducting income tax under the Pay As You Earn scheme and a range of other beneficial information.

WAGES RECORD BOOK

When employing staff you will need a **wages record book**. The employee will receive a pay advice slip which you will either give to her with her wages, or if you pay directly into her bank account, you will give the employee a pay advice on its own. A pay advice slip could look like the one opposite:

You should record all the details in the **wages book** – it will be required by your accountant.

INCOME TAX

The Employer's Quick Guide to PAYE and NICS.CWGI April 1998 provides **all** the necessary information for employing staff. As an **employer** you are responsible for operating **PAYE**, you will:

- inform the tax office when your employee starts;
- deduct tax from your employee's wages according to tax tables supplied by the Inland Revenue;
- pay the tax deducted to the IR monthly;
- complete the tax cards issued by the IR which record all the information relating to your employee's wages;
- tell the tax office when the employee leaves your employment.

When your employee leaves you will complete **Form P.45**. This shows:

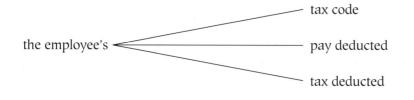

the employee's — tax code

the employee's — pay deducted

the employee's — tax deducted

PAY ADVICE SLIP

Name ....

Week No .... Date ....

Basic pay	£
Overtime	£
Commission	£
Bonuses	
Total gross pay (before deductions)	£
Income tax	£
NI	£
Other	£
Total deductions	£
Total net pay (after deductions)	£

Figure 12.1 Sample pay advice slip

throughout the year she has worked to the leaving date. One part of this form goes to the tax office; the other part goes to the new employer.

P60
At the end of each tax year the employee receives a P60 which details the **Tax, N.I.** and any other information relating to the wages.

Tax codes
All employees under the PAYE system are issued with a tax code. If your employee has been previously employed she will give you a P.45 which will give you this information. If not, she must apply to the tax office for a code.

A new employee, who has not paid tax before, will have a P46 issued by the tax office. Once signed by the employer the tax office will issue an **emergency code**.

The tax code gives one certain allowances. Everyone is entitled to a **personal allowance**. This is the amount they are allowed to earn before paying tax. It is usually raised each year in the government's budget. For example if your allowances are £4,335 (the current single person's allowance), your code would be 344. A letter usually follows this code: L is a common one and it includes the personal allowance for those aged under 65.

For more information on the **Inland Revenue and Tax Codes** (refer to the Employer's Quick guide).

NATIONAL INSURANCE

When you employ people you are responsible for paying their wages and also deducting income tax and national insurance (NI) contributions. NI contributions provide a range of benefits including unemployment, statutory sick pay, state pensions, industrial disability.

For more information refer to 'Inland Revenue and the Contributions Agency' (Employer's Quick Guide).

You or your accountant can work out how much NI must be deducted by the tables supplied in the Quick Guide.

if you are a sole trader you will have
to pay Class 2 NI contributions

|

if your business is a company, then you are
an employee and you will pay Class 1 contributions

|

if you employ staff, then they will pay Class 1
contributions if they earn more than the Lower
Earnings Limit

What you need to know

There are *four* classes of contribution:

Class 1

This is paid by employers and their employees between the age of 16 and retirement (60 for a woman and 65 for a man) when earnings reach the Lower Earnings Limit.

> Class 2

This is a 'flat-rate' amount paid by self-employed people. You can only claim exemption if your earnings fall below a specified level in the tax year.

> Class 3

These are voluntary contributions paid at a flat-rate per week. These are available for people who have paid too few Class 1 or 2 contributions to qualify for state benefit.

> Class 4

This might also be paid by the self-employed person if her/his taxable profit is over a certain amount (check current legislation). This additional payment is assessed and collected by the Inland Revenue. Only half of the Class 4 contribution is payable as tax relief is given on the other half.

> A certificate of exemption

This can be applied for (in advance only) if you think that your earnings from self-employment will be below the Lower Earnings Limit.

How to pay NI
NI can be paid monthly at a Post Office or by direct debit from a bank account.

STATUTORY SICK PAY (SSP)

When employing staff you must pay a minimum level of sick pay to most employees aged 16 or over, if this has been specified in the contract of employment. If they have been off sick for four or more days in a row and up to 28 weeks. After this time State Benefit starts and your liability ceases.

- you pay SSP like normal pay;
- you can claim back most of the SSP each month from you NI contributions or tax payments.

For current rates refer to: **Statutory Sick Pay** in Employer's Quick Guide to **PAYE and NICS.CWGI April 1998** available from your local DSS who also operate an advice line for employers – 0345 143 143.

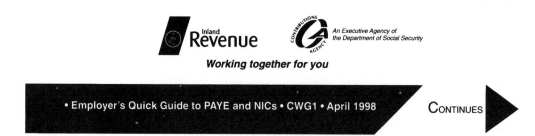

Introduction

CONTENTS LIST AND HELPFUL INFORMATION

These cards are for use from 6 April 1998 and replace the 1997 edition

Card number	Title	Card number	Title
Introduction	Contents list and Helpful information	12	P11 - Completion for PAYE in K code cases
1	PAYE and NICs - general	13	Company directors - NICs
2	PAYE codes and Tax Tables	14	Class 1A NICs on cars and fuel
3	Using the Pay Adjustment Tables - Tax Tables A	15	Class 1A NICs - Keeping records and how to pay - Fuel scale - Calculation example.
4	How to work out NICs		
5	Rates and information for the 1998/99 Tax Year (6 April 1998 to 5 April 1999)	16	Statutory Sick Pay
6	National Insurance numbers, computer payrolls and payroll agents	17	Statutory Maternity Pay
		18	What to do at the end of each tax month
7	New employee	19	Completing - End of Year Returns (1997/98) - End of Year Summary, P14(OCR)
8	P46 procedures		
9	P11 - Deductions Working Sheet for PAYE and NICs - Completion for NICs.	20	Example of a completed P35
10	P11 - Completion for PAYE	21	P14(OCR) - completed example. What to do when an employee stops working for you. P45 - completed example
11	P11 - Examples of both PAYE and NICs entries		

If you are unhappy with our service

If you are unhappy with any aspect of the service you get please tell us.

For matters relating to NICs
Contact the Contributions Manager at the office you have been dealing with or ask for leaflet *Unhappy with our Service?* CA62, available from your local Social Security office.

For matters relating to PAYE
Contact the Officer in Charge at your PAYE Tax Office or ask for leaflet *You and the Inland Revenue,* IR120.

Inland **Revenue** An Executive Agency of the Department of Social Security

Working together for you

• Employer's Quick Guide to PAYE and NICs • CWG1 • April 1998   CONTINUES ▶

Figure 12.2 Employer's Quick Guide

<table>
<tr><td>**8**</td><td>P46 PROCEDURES</td><td>**8**</td></tr>
</table>

Completing form P46

Card 7 tells you when you should use this card.

If you are making pension payments please see the *Employer's Further Guide to PAYE and NICs*, CWG2 under 'pensions'.

When you are following the form P46 procedure:

- ask the employee for their National Insurance number. Card 6 explains why the National Insurance Number is important and how to get it
- give the employee form P46 and ask the employee to:
  - read statements A, B and C
  - tick each box that applies
  - sign and date the form if appropriate
  - complete the slip at the bottom of the form
- fill in the rest of the form
- look at the chart overleaf to find out what to do next

An example of a completed form P46

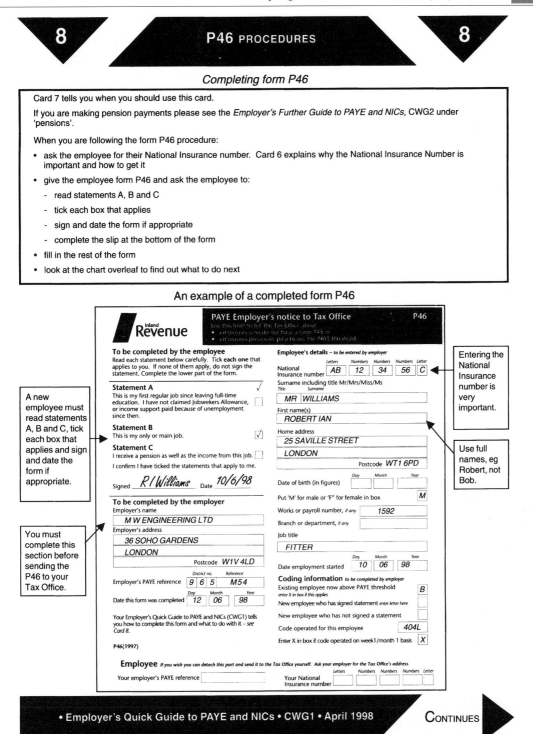

A new employee must read statements A, B and C, tick each box that applies and sign and date the form if appropriate.

You must complete this section before sending the P46 to your Tax Office.

Entering the National Insurance number is very important.

Use full names, eg Robert, not Bob.

16 STATUTORY SICK PAY **16**

This side of the card gives you background information. There is a checklist on the reverse for how to work out Statutory Sick Pay.

Introduction

Statutory Sick Pay (SSP) is the minimum level of sick pay you must pay to most employees who are off work sick for 4 or more calendar days in a row. It is paid for qualifying days (after an employee has served 3 waiting days) for employees with average weekly earnings of not less than the lower earnings limit for the payment of NICs.

This card outlines the basic facts about the calculation and payment of SSP. If you need further information, please consult the *Statutory Sick Pay and Statutory Maternity Pay Tables*, CA35/36, or the *Manual for Employers on Statutory Sick Pay*, CA30, from April 1997 and the April 1998 Supplement to that manual.

The reverse of the 'Introduction' card under 'What if I need further information or help?...' tells you how to get these Tables/Manuals.

From 6 April 1997 you may choose whether or not to operate a lot of the rules of the Statutory Sick Pay scheme **but only** if you pay contractual remuneration, e.g. wages, occupational sick pay etc to an employee at or above the SSP rate. However, you will still need to keep basic records.

For further details, see the CA30 under 'Freedom from SSP scheme'.

Who qualifies for Statutory Sick Pay?.....

SSP should be paid to the majority of employees who:

1 are aged 16 or over and under 65

2 are off work for 4 or more calendar days in a row. This is a Period of Incapacity for Work (PIW), and

3 in the 8 weeks prior to being off work, have average weekly earnings of not less than the lower earnings limit for the payment of NICs

SSP does not have to be paid if, on the first day of the PIW, an employee:

1 does not satisfy the previous conditions,

2 has already received 28 weeks SSP in the PIW

3 has not yet done any work for you

4 is within the disqualifying period of her pregnancy, or

5 has claimed Social Security benefit that links with the PIW

For details of more unusual circumstances in which SSP is not payable, see the CA30 under 'Employee who cannot get SSP'.

If an employee does not qualify for a payment of SSP, you must complete form SSP1. This form will enable the employee to claim Incapacity Benefit. If you need more information, see the CA30 under 'Forms, SSP1'. Form SSP1 can be obtained from the Contributions Agency via your local Social Security Office.

When liability to pay Statutory Sick Pay ends

SSP is payable for a maximum of 28 weeks within the PIW. Liability to pay ceases on the sooner of:

• the employee returning to work

• the employee leaving your employment

• the employee ceasing to send in doctor's certificates

• the maximum 28 weeks' payment have been made

• the start of her maternity pay period.

For further information see the CA30 under 'When Statutory Sick Pay ends'.

If the employee leaves your employment, and SSP was payable in at least 1 of the 8 weeks prior to the contract of service ending, you should issue a *Leaver's Statement* form SSP1(L) if the employee requests it. For further information see the CA30 under 'Forms, SSP1(L)'.

Claiming back Statutory Sick Pay

If you qualify, under the Percentage Threshold Scheme (PTS), you are entitled to recover a certain amount of SSP paid to your employees.

To see if you can recover any SSP under the PTS, you must compare the total SSP paid in a tax month with 13% of the **gross** Class 1 National Insurance contributions payable for the same tax month. You can recover any SSP amount which exceeds the 13% figure.

You should not use entries recorded on the Employers Payment Record, form P32, as a basis for calculating the Class 1 NICs and SSP paid in a tax month. This is because the form is not split into **actual** tax months.

For more information about recovering SSP, see the CA30 under 'Recovering SSP'.

• Employer's Quick Guide to PAYE and NICs • CWG1 • April 1998

CONTINUES

PENSION SCHEME OR STAKEHOLDER PENSION

As a salon owner you will want to plan for your retirement. A personal pension will enable you to do this. A further incentive is the tax relief that you are eligible to claim if you pay income tax. You may also want to help your staff with this.

After 2001 as a salon owner and employer you will be required to make available a **Stakeholder Pension** to employees if you do not offer a pension scheme, but you **do not** have to contribute to the scheme on behalf of the employees. This is because in December 1998 the Government planned Pension Reform to replace the State Earnings Related Pension Scheme (SERPS).

Further information can be obtained from companies such as **Abbey Life**

Self Assessments and Activities

1 List the necessary deductions on a pay advice slip.

2 Under the PAYE tax system, an individual is given a personal tax code. Find out how this is calculated.

3 As a salon owner, which class of NI contribution would:

(a) you pay;

(b) your employee pay.

4 From where would you obtain advice on tax codes?

5 From where would you obtain advice on NI?

6 Obtain details of a personal pension plan from two companies.

7 Explain the importance of a **P. 60**.

8 From where would you obtain advice on sick pay?

9 Identify the different classes of National Insurance contribution.

CHAPTER 13

Staff training

OBJECTIVES

This chapter explains the importance of primary accounts and money transactions that your staff will need to know in order to assist in running your business. A working knowledge of purchase orders, delivery notes, goods received notes, invoices, credit notes, debit notes, statements of accounts is given. The importance of keeping accurate stock records for stock turnover and annual stocktaking is also explained.

Money transactions – cash, cheque and credit cards – require different handling, and staff need to be proficient in making accurate transactions. The Cheques Act 1992 makes payment by cheque safer than before.

EFFECTIVE SALON RECORDS

If they are to assist you well in the running of your business, your staff will need to be familiar with the following:

purchase orders

|

delivery notes

|

goods received notes

|

invoices

|

credit notes

|

debit notes

|

statements of account

A regular weekly session could be the best time to offer on-going training in your salon. You might prepare sample sheets and keep them in a training manual. *Keep it simple.*

> A purchase order

is when you complete a form to buy products from another supplier/company.

> Delivery notes

or a goods received note is given to the salon when goods ordered are delivered. Delivery notes should be checked carefully with the products to make sure they have all been delivered. Sometimes the delivery note may not show all the articles if the supplier was out of stock. The products should also be checked to make sure they are in good condition. The receiver usually signs a delivery note; a copy of this is kept by the receiver and one by the person delivering the goods.

When the goods have been delivered:

> The invoice

will be sent. This is a bill and must be checked against the delivery note and then paid. Many suppliers allow up to 30 days' credit.

> A credit note

is received when there has been an overpayment at some time and the supplier is advising you of this.

> A debit note

order form

43 Bayton Road, Exhall, Coventry, CV7 9EF

Purchase Order Number: 1007

Personal Account Reference Number: A B T 9 0 0

Name: A Beauty Therapist   Address... N° 2 Any Street,
Any Town   Post Code: ATO 000 Tel No: 00123 45678

enclose my cheque for £ 72-00 or wish to pay by credit card   Card Type:

Card No.

Expiry Date: ...../.............../...........

switch issue number

Date ..../.............../...........

CREDIT CARD HOLDERS name and address MUST be filled in below if different from above:

Name: Address:

Code   Tel No:...........................

Cat. Code	Description	Colour/Size	Qty	Price Each	Total
WE253	100 PAPER WAXING STRIPS	—	6	2-25	13-50
DC950	LION DE-LUXE PAPER ROLL 10"	—	4	1-50	6-00
WT505	DUELL GOLD TEA TREE KIT	—	1	45-00	45-00

order line: 01203 361619

TOPS order line: 01203 644654

fax order line: 01203 644010

email order line: sales@ellisons.co.uk

Sub Total	64-50
Less 5% Prompt Payment	61-28
Plus Postage/Carriage	Free
Plus VAT @ 17.5%	10-72
Total	72-00

Please despatch my order (signed) A Bth   Date 08.07.99 Sales Executive:

Normal Terms and Conditions apply as shown overleaf.

Figure 13.1 Sample Purchase Order

is when the salon owes the supplier. When a salon buys from a particular supplier on a regular basis, the salon will have an account with the supplier. The supplier will issue a statement of account at the end of each month.

> A statement of account

will show:

- the amount that has been **ordered**;
- the amount that has been **paid**;
- the amount that is **outstanding**.

INVOICES

An invoice might look like this:

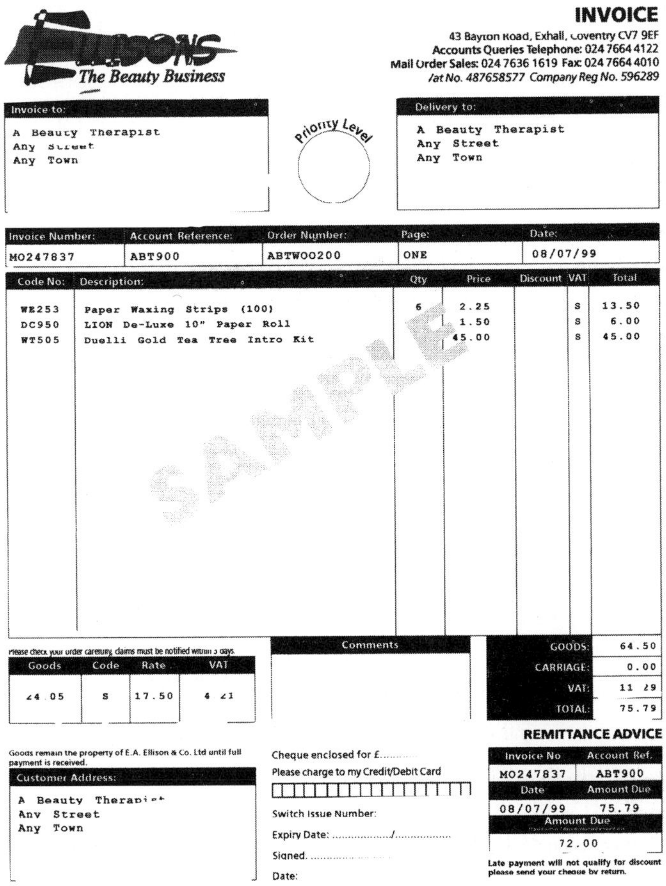

INVOICE

43 Bayton Road, Exhall, Coventry CV7 9EF
Accounts Queries Telephone: 024 7664 4122
Mail Order Sales: 024 7636 1619 Fax: 024 7664 4010
Vat No. 487658577 Company Reg No. 596289

Ellisons The Beauty Business

Invoice to:
A Beauty Therapist
Any Street
Any Town

Priority Level

Delivery to:
A Beauty Therapist
Any Street
Any Town

Invoice Number:	Account Reference:	Order Number:	Page:	Date:
MO247837	ABT900	ABTWO0200	ONE	08/07/99

Code No:	Description:	Qty	Price	Discount	VAT	Total
WE253	Paper Waxing Strips (100)	6	2.25		S	13.50
DC950	LION De-Luxe 10" Paper Roll		1.50		S	6.00
WT505	Duelli Gold Tea Tree Intro Kit		45.00		S	45.00

SAMPLE

Please check your order carefully, claims must be notified within 3 days.

Goods	Code	Rate	VAT
64.05	S	17.50	4 21

Comments

GOODS:	64.50
CARRIAGE:	0.00
VAT:	11 29
TOTAL:	75.79

Goods remain the property of E.A. Ellison & Co. Ltd until full payment is received.

Customer Address:
A Beauty Therapist
Any Street
Any Town

Cheque enclosed for £........
Please charge to my Credit/Debit Card
Switch Issue Number:
Expiry Date: ..../................
Signed. ....
Date:

REMITTANCE ADVICE

Invoice No	Account Ref.
MO247837	ABT900
Date	Amount Due
08/07/99	75.79

Amount Due
72.00

Late payment will not qualify for discount please send your cheque by return.

Figure 13.2 Sample invoice

STOCK TURNOVER

This is an important factor in your business:

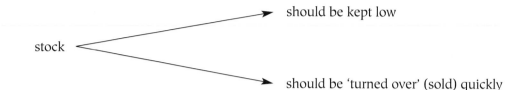

stock
→ should be kept low
→ should be 'turned over' (sold) quickly

When the stock is sold quickly, cash is available and your money is being used properly. Your daily analysis in the cash book will show you the products and services which are selling well. If sales fall, then you must reduce your stock purchasing as well.

STOCK RECORDS

Stock can be recorded when your order arrives simply by keeping a stock record book. An example of a **simple stock record**:

Date	Supplier	Received	Balance	Sold
10.07.00	Breens order No.24	10	18	8

Figure 13.3 Sample stock record book

Every **category of produce** will have a **column** and information from your purchase records will ensure it is accurate. Similarly, **records of sales** are necessary.

Accurate **records of sales** and **purchases** are needed for your end-of-year accounts and you will have to stocktake for this purpose.

If you **use a computer** in your salon, **this information** can be **recorded on a regular basis**. The computer package you use will:
- record the information;
- calculate your stock;
- forecast your requirements.

STOCKTAKE

You will be required to *stocktake* your stock assets for your accounting year. This means that you will have to count your stock and value it. If a computer package is used, this will be a simple matter of pressing a few buttons and the results will appear if you have accurately recorded up-to-date information.

If you undertake this task manually, it can take a considerable time. However, if your stock control record books are kept up to date, this will save time and energy.

MONEY TRANSACTIONS

Your clients will pay by:

- cash;
- cheque;
- credit card;
- debit card;

Your staff should be proficient in handling all these transactions.

Cash

This is the simplest transaction as long as the therapist or receptionist is proficient in giving change. You will probably have an electronic till which will save any problems, as it will:

- separate information (itemise bill);
- add up the bill;
- show the correct change;
- issue a receipt;
- show up any errors.

In addition the till will total the day's takings and collate various information that you require. It is also a safe, secure method of storing money (refer page 152).

Cheques

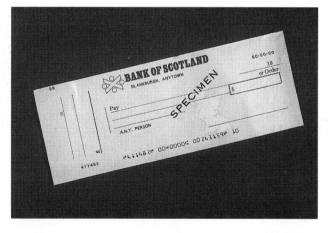

Figure 13.4 A sample cheque

The Cheques Act 1992 aimed to make cheques safer as a means of payment by reducing fraud. It advised that cheques crossed with the words: 'Account Payee' or 'Account Payee only' ('A/C Payee' or 'A/C Payee only') cannot normally be transferred to another person. Such a cheque must be paid into an account in the name of the person named in the 'pay' section of the cheque. Your staff will need to check these points:

- the date should be correct;
- the cheque should be made out to the retailer;
- the amount in words should match the amount in figures;

- the cheque must be signed by the person paying at that time;
- the client should have a current cheque card which guarantees the cheque up to a certain limit, for example, £100 (the bank does not have to honour a cheque above this amount);
- the card also shows the client's signature and the cheque card number and the card expiry date should be written on the back of the cheque (by the therapist/receptionist).

If these points are checked, then your payment by cheque will be received.

 Remember → check now, payment later
miss now, *miss out!*

Credit cards

Mastercard and Barclaycard/VISA are two well-known credit cards. These services cost you – the retailer. As a service charge, you pay a small percentage of the value of your sale. The salon owner also pays a sum to join the scheme. This can be expensive for you when starting your business.

- The client who uses the card gains a period of credit.
- You present the bill to the bank and you receive payment.

There are still manual machines for processing payment by credit card and your staff would need to be proficient in carrying out a transaction, but these are generally being replaced by automatic transaction machines.

Your salon would need a terminal (a portable electronic machine) and the credit card is inserted, 'swiped', and details are checked and cleared at the central computer. (EFTPOS Electronic Funds Transfer at Point of Sale). When authorisation follows the transaction is then processed by the terminal and the credit card sales slip is printed. This method is safer than the manual machines which are unable to give authorisation. You would need to check by telephone if you wanted to know this.

Debit cards

Switch/Delta/Connect

This method of payment means that payment is made automatically by electronic transfer from the client's bank account.

Self Assessments and Activities

1 You are making a staff information manual for use in your salon. Prepare a few sample pages, clearly and concisely, showing some of the information you would include.

2 Design a stock record card that you might use in your salon.

3 Prepare a simple instruction guide to show staff how to record 'stock records' accurately.

4 Explain the terms

a) stock turnover

b) stocktake.

5 Prepare a list of incentives you would offer your staff.

CHAPTER 14

Staff appraisal

OBJECTIVES

This chapter explains the importance of regularly monitoring staff performance through appraisal. Appraisal means that the employer can identify training needs, assess job satisfaction, target goals, highlight problems, develop good communication skills and understanding. The employee has the opportunity to evaluate her performance, discuss problems and career aims and to feel valued. The appraiser will need to use good communication skills and an objective, honest, open approach in order for the appraisal to be meaningful. An appraisee performance form should be completed by the appraisee and appraiser for future appraisals.

Well-conducted appraisals can improve staff relations and assist in identifying an individual's needs, performance, strengths and weaknesses. They assist you – the salon owner – in identifying training needs, skill shortages, employees' needs and your salon's needs.

In the year 2000, industry has become very aware of the importance of training and career development. If your business is to meet and maintain high standards of professional expertise, it is necessary to employ motivated staff and to keep them motivated.

The *purpose* of appraisal is:
1. **To assess the individual's performance**
- technical skills
- strengths
- weaknesses
- future aims
- promotional potential
- areas for improvement

- further training needs and encouraging:
- self-assessment/evaluation
- job satisfaction
2. **To allow you to:**
- give and gain information
- improve communication skills
- give praise and constructive advice
- show personal interest
- identify training needs
- target future goals
- identify individual needs
- identify areas for attention
- maintain a productive working environment
- achieve staff satisfaction.

You will need to **conduct the appraisal in private**. That means:

- a quiet place
- with sufficient time for the interview.

Your approach and attitude is very important.

You will need to **demonstrate good supervisory skills**. You want your appraisee to:

- relax
- talk freely
- be honest.

You must adopt a similar manner and ensure that you are:

- friendly
- open
- objective
- positive.

Some appraisals may need particular skills and all demand **excellent communication skills**.

You may have an appraisee who has a variety of weaknesses:

- lateness
- poor work record
- poor attitude.

You will need to:

- present the facts
- ask for reasons
- listen.

Your employee will be able to:

- discuss problems;
- air grievances;
- discuss her career aims;
- discuss her strengths and weaknesses;

- measure her performance;
- see that you take a personal interest in her.

As an employer, you will be able to:

- improve communication skills and understanding;
- identify staff training needs;
- assess job satisfaction among staff;
- discuss the strengths and weaknesses of staff;
- target goals for the future;
- identify objectives to enhance performance;
- highlight areas that need attention among staff;
- offer constructive advice and praise to staff;
- show your employees that you care and are interested in their career development.

As an employer how you **approach** the appraisal is very important – you should **value** the opportunity to **talk** with your staff and **listen** to their **needs** and **identify** their strengths and weaknesses and their career aims.

You should use an easy approach to accomplish this. If you are a 'good' employer, true appraisal is operating continuously. A few periods set aside throughout the year would be to discuss points in depth.

Your manner needs to be:
- honest;
- positive;
- objective;
- open;
- friendly;
- calm;

so that your employee is encouraged to talk freely.

If you know that some of your comments might not be favourable, you should make sure that you:

have full employee information available

|

state any problems clearly

|

always back up with facts

|

ask for reasons

|

listen

|

agree on action

EMPLOYEE PERFORMANCE ASSESSMENT

Date
Name of employee (appraisee)
Job title
Date employment commenced
Date started in present position
Date of last appraisal
Date of next appraisal – review date

Assessment Rating 1–5

1. unacceptable – does not meet the requirements of the position
2. below average — improvement necessary
3. satisfactory – developing
4. effective
5. excellent/outstanding

Areas to be Assessed
Communication Skills

	RATING	COMMENTS
Clients		
Staff		
Manner		
Verbal		
Non-verbal		
Team member		

Job Performance/Competencies

	RATING	COMMENTS
Treatment/technical skills		
Salon organisation		
Sales		
Targets		
Supervisory (if applicable)		

Personal Application

	RATING	COMMENTS
Time-keeping		
Time-off (sickness)		
Appearance		
Attitude		
Motivation		
Confidence		
Initiative		
Job satisfaction		

Overall Rating ☐ **Comments**

Training and Development Plan

On-going training or support training/targets
Identify objectives to enhance performance

Action Plan

Review date

Short term targets
Long term targets

Signature Appraisee ....
Appraiser ....
Comments on appraisal ....
....

To be given to appraisee one week before the appraisal and then given to the appraiser

Name ....

Appraisee – Self-Evaluation

Assess your strengths and weaknesses in your position

Consider any support training or further training that you would need to develop yourself.

Future Career Aims

Plan Of Action

To be completed after the appraisal

Your Views On This Appraisal

Signature

You should also ensure when you conduct the appraisal that:

- it is private;
- there are no interruptions;
- you concentrate on problems/situations that can be improved;
- you agree on an action plan and target;
- you identify training areas which may be needed to achieve certain objectives.

An appraisal form should have information you think necessary to monitor progress. A few useful guidelines are suggested on pages 128–30

An appraisal interview takes time – **ensure sufficient time is allowed**. A well-conducted appraisal can improve staff relations and will assist your employee in her development and assist you in the running of your salon.

Appraisals help to develop **your staff**

Developing your staff is *identifying*

their needs
|
performance
|
weaknesses
|
strengths
|
needs for training

Successful, satisfied staff work well and develop your business.

Appraisals assist *you* to identify

areas for training
|
skill shortages
|
problems – before they get too big
|
your employee's needs
|
your salon's needs

Self Assessments and Activities

1 Appraisal is an important process, give five reasons why you agree.

2 List the qualities of an appraiser.

3 Create a simulation of the 'appraiser' and 'appraisee'.

4 Design an appropriate form that might be used in an appraisal.

CHAPTER 15

Salon layout and design

OBJECTIVES

This chapter explains salon layout and design. There are companies that can assist you with planning your salon. When setting up a salon, consideration must be given to the reception area, staff areas, store rooms, therapy rooms, changing rooms, heating and ventilation, showers and toilets as well as colour schemes, floor covering, fixtures/fittings and equipment.

WHERE TO GET ADVICE

There are companies who will advise on salon layout. This is often free of charge if you purchase equipment from them.

HOF (House of Famuir) offers salon planning on the basis of a fee, currently £70 + VAT. HOF produces a suggested layout based on:

■ the size of salon;
■ what you envisage in the salon;

- the type of treatments intended;
- the number of therapists, and so on.

HOF does not produce architectural drawings, as these are a matter for the salon owner's builders/architects.

Some other companies which give informal advice on equipment and planning are Ellisons and Taylor Reeson.

> Don't forget, look around and see what companies can offer you.

SETTING UP THE SALON

Before you start to plan your salon it is a very useful exercise to visit a few salons and have some beauty treatments. You can 'enjoy' the treatments and at the same time put yourself in a client situation.

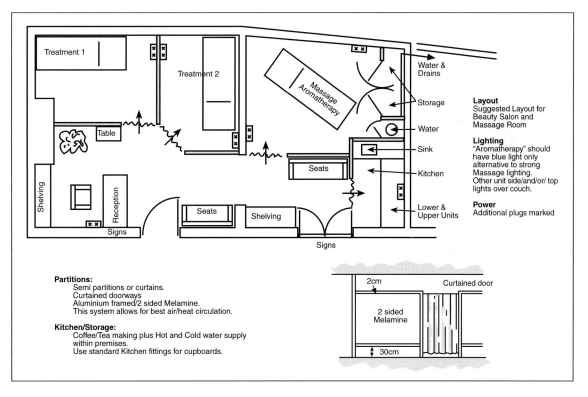

Figure 15.1 Suggested layout for beauty salon and massage room (submitted by HOF)

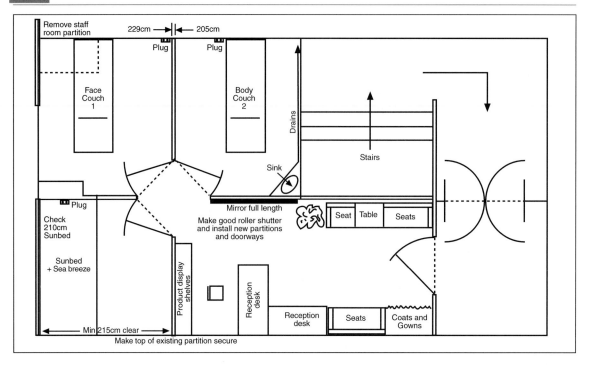

Figure 15.2 Suggested layout for beauty salon (submitted by HOF)

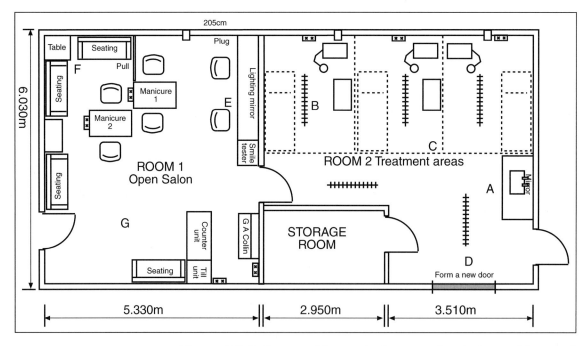

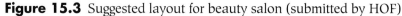

Figure 15.3 Suggested layout for beauty salon (submitted by HOF)

Ask yourself

Did I:

- like the reception area?
- was it, attractive, crowded?
- were the changing areas crowded?
- was the treatment room claustrophobic, relaxing?
- was the decor suitable?
- was there too much noise?
- was the lighting too bright?
- was it a clean, fresh, safe and inviting salon?

Planning your salon means that you must consider:

- staff comfort and efficiency;
- your clients' comfort;
- meeting current legislation, that is, various Acts which stipulate how you operate your working environment.

The salon layout is often dependent on the existing plumbing. You may wish to change this or add to it – it will depend on your financial budget. Once you have organised your 'wet' areas, you will want to consider **your layout**.

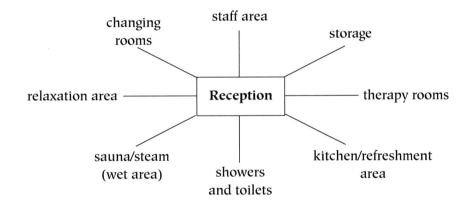

The most important area of a salon is the **reception** – it is where your client arrives. If this area is dull, uninteresting, crowded and your client is badly received, she will not return. **Your reception area will need:**

comfortable chairs
|
a table
|
product display units
|
a magazine area
|

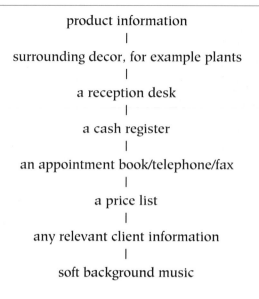

product information

|

surrounding decor, for example plants

|

a reception desk

|

a cash register

|

an appointment book/telephone/fax

|

a price list

|

any relevant client information

|

soft background music

You will need to have a suitable area near here to place the client's coat. Your client needs to feel welcomed and made at ease as quickly as possible.

Your **business registration certificate** should be displayed in the reception area if you are a limited company, so should a **disclaimer notice**, that is to show that you cannot take responsibility for the security of clients' property. It is also compulsory to display **a list of your charges**; your **diplomas** and your staff's diplomas should also be exhibited. The changing rooms should be discreet and private, that is, not in view of the reception area, and the beauty therapy rooms will require:

electrical points

|

space

|

cupboards

|

shelving

|

lighting

|

equipment

THERAPY ROOMS

You may choose to have one room for waxing, one for epilation and one for general treatments. In which instance you can design each for its purpose. But it may not be possible to specify your rooms if you are to be cost effective. So that means that the rooms must be easily adaptable. Trol-

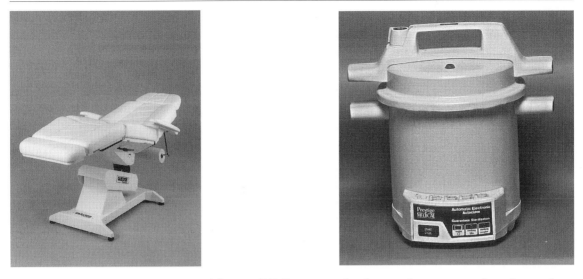

Figure 15.4 Essential salon equipment: couch and autoclave

leys can be very useful and can be prepared in advance for waxing and electrolysis and other treatments. They can offer a simple alternative. Whatever you decide you will want your therapy room to be clean, safe and comfortable.

You will need to be able to move around the couch and all equipment will need to be easily accessible. The size of your equipment will determine the space you need in the therapy room particularly if you have a multi-purpose unit. There should be adequate electrical points so that the equipment can be used safely with a minimum of lead exposed.

Areas that are purpose designed mean that everything is
- easy to reach;
- easy to move;
- easy to clean;
- easy for safe handling.

A work-surface shelf can be a good idea with suitable shelves for storage below, but dust covers are necessary to protect equipment and keep products protected. You may prefer a storage cupboard where everything is packed away and the cupboard surface is designed as a work-surface. **A wash basin should be nearby and a suitable covered** bin for general waste and a **'sharps' container for used electrolysis needles and micro-lancers**.

Apart from colour co-ordinated towels and couch covering you will need disposable material such as couch rolls which usually fit on the end of the couch and paper towels, tissues, paper capes, paper slippers. Where possible **materials should be disposable**.

You will need a trolley for the materials and products that the therapist will be using but there should also be products displayed for the client to see and ask questions about them before and after treatment. **Sales start in the treatment room.**

LIGHTING

Localised lighting, on a stand, can be extremely useful because it is portable, efficient and only used when required. Overhead lighting needs to be controllable i.e. using a dimmer control; because bright lights are not suitable for relaxing treatments. Some concealed lighting can be very effective for creating space in the salon as well as adding a warm glow. Where it is possible daylight is a useful, economical asset in a salon.

Mirrors also complement lighting but careful placement is important in order to create the right effect.

DECOR

The *colour scheme* for the salon will be dependent on your own taste, but it is good to consider:
- colours that will not date;
- colours that harmonise and create a relaxed atmosphere.

Good colour co-ordination will please any age group. Pastel colours are popular for this reason. Advice on colour and fabric matching can be obtained from department stores. Changes in colour schemes can be quite simple if you consider this at the beginning.

Pink is often a popular colour and is very soothing, but it is also thought of as a feminine colour. Male clients will also visit your salon so colours need to suit both sexes.

Peach and pale gold are colours that are 'warm' and can have a vivid colour such as terracotta or deep amber to contrast, perhaps one wall or some soft furnishings e.g. curtains. You may decide on a neutral colour such as cream, which is not as stark as white and offers a good opportunity to use bright colours for your soft furnishings and salon wear. It is important to consider the whole salon decor, and include gowns, towels, couch covering and staff uniforms. You will want to select colours that blend well together and give your salon a state of the art image.

Your walls should be easily washable to ensure a high standard of cleanliness and plain walls allow greater flexibility. You may consider paintings or photographs for the wall. They could complement your work in some areas e.g. make-up, advertising a product and they could be for rest and relaxation e.g. a sea scene or a country scene. Pictures need to blend in with the decor, the frame and the colours in the picture. Whatever colour you select be sure that you can mix and match it if you want to change your colour scheme at a later date.

HYGIENE

Hygiene is vital in the beauty salon and your **floor covering** will receive a lot of attention. It needs to be:

- comfortable to stand on;
- non-slip;
- hardwearing and able to withstand floor cleansers.

Good flooring is expensive but necessary if it is to meet the demands of everyday use. **Carpet is not a good idea for beauty therapy rooms**, although it is attractive for your reception area.

Your soft furnishings e.g. curtains will need to be of a fabric that can be washed and will withstand regular washing and still look good (i.e. not shrink or fade).

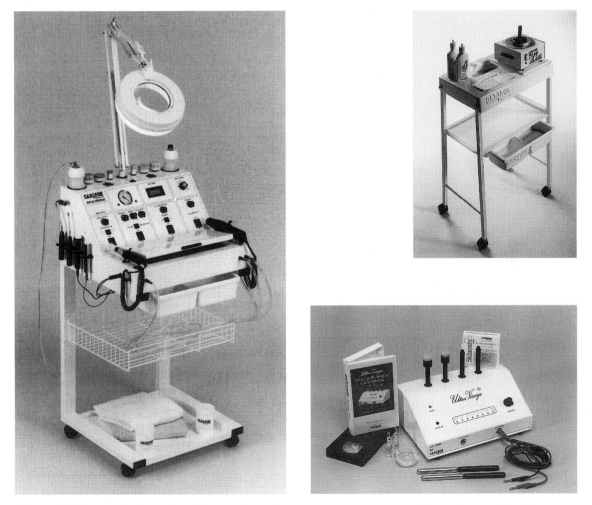

Figure 15.5 A selection of equipment for salon use: microcurrent, waxing trolley and facial system

FIXTURES, FITTINGS AND EQUIPMENT

You will need to consider these carefully and will probably change your mind a number of times. For this reason it is important to ensure that your fittings, where possible, are adaptable and that some equipment is portable so that maximum output is possible. Seek advice from the professionals and consider your own particular requirements before you rush into this area of planning. Equipment needs to be:

- reliable;
- repairable.

Check with suppliers if they offer:

- a repair service;
- a free loan while an item is being repaired.

 **REMEMBER**

All equipment must carry the **CE** marking which is the common quality standard of the EU. The equipment may also carry the **BSI** (British Standards Institute) mark – the '**kitemark**' but the manufacturer's offer their products to the BSI for testing/marking on a voluntary basis.

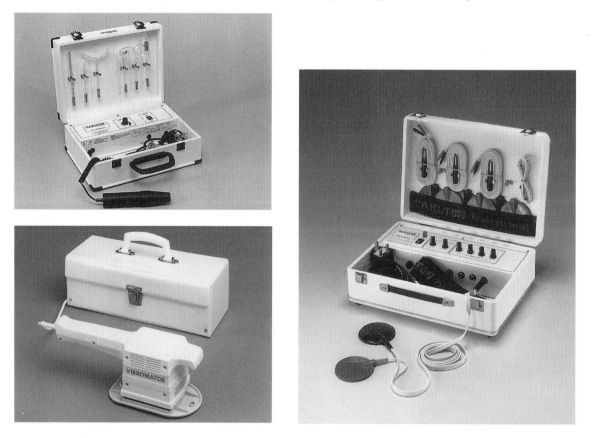

Figure 15.6 A selection of portable equipment: high frequency, Faradic and massager

SECOND-HAND EQUIPMENT

This can be useful for 'furniture' requirements, including tables, couches and stools. New electrical equipment comes with a guarantee – this must be considered when setting-up a salon.

Cost is also a key factor. Before you buy:
- check out the wholesalers;
- check out the equipment;
- check out the service.

STORE ROOM

Store rooms should be in an area that is easily accessible for staff, but not near client areas.

You will need a cupboard for salon and retail products. It will need to be
- secure;
- have adequate shelving;
- fulfil your needs.

All products should be clearly marked (see page 156) and comply with COSHH regulations (see page 44).

A storage cupboard would also be needed for products and items for everyday salon use, such as:
- client gowns;
- towels;
- couch rolls.

A separate cupboard should be used for salon cleaning materials and **dangerous substances** must be stored in a metal cupboard in case of fire. These cupboards need to be accessible but, not in public view. They need to be **well maintained** at all times. Large salons may choose to have a fully-equipped storage cupboard in each working area. It will depend on your needs.

HEATING AND VENTILATION

This is necessary if your salon is to function properly and to comply with legislation. **Seek professional advice on efficiency and performance and safety**.

 REMEMBER
The salon can generate a lot of heat with various treatments and an even temperature is desirable for working therapists and client comfort.

STAFF AREA

This should be designed according to current legislation (see page 47).

Your staff should have an area to change their clothes and to put their personal belongings whilst they are working.

Staff will also need to take their breaks and relax in this area when they are not working.

TOILET FACILITIES

It is necessary to have separate toilet facilities for staff and clients (see current legislation page 47).

CLIENT COMFORT

When considering client comfort, give them the feeling of luxury and being pampered. Think about:

■ changing rooms;
■ toilets;
■ shower areas;
■ steam baths;
■ saunas.

A salon that has been designed carefully allows the client to progress from changing room to treatment area with a simple, on-going progression in a relaxed, private environment.

REFRESHMENT AREA

This is subject to the Food Hygiene Regulations and local authority Environmental Health Act. You may choose to use a vending machine or to serve your clients. Personal attention and the use of cups and saucers is still favoured by many clients as 'elegant', giving them the feeling of luxury and being pampered. You must consider all aspects when making your decision to serve refreshments:

hygiene
|
cost
|
space
|
clientele

THE SALON'S EXTERIOR

Your salon's exterior image must be inviting and attractive. It is really saying 'this place is for you, come in'.

You will probably want to have:

- a new canopy;
- your own sign and logo.

What you want and what you have will depend on:

- your budget;
- council legislation.

REMEMBER
Always check legislation before you make plans as it can save disappointment and money.

THE SALON'S INTERIOR

The interior of your salon will develop as you decorate and furnish it. You will need to consider the finishing touches and any extras that may enhance your salon.

Plants

A few plants can add life and colour, but make sure that they are always well-maintained.

Silk flower displays

These need to be washed regularly (real flowers are not advisable because clients may have allergies).

Pictures/Photographs

(See page 138.)

Statues

Statues can enhance the environment if it blends with the decor and if you have sufficient space.

Centre pieces

They could be water display units with lights. They can be very attractive but you do need space and they can be noisy.

A music system

This can set the scene for a relaxing environment and the music should be gentle, quiet and not obtrusive. Loud dominating music will not create a relaxed environment.

Remember
If you play music in a public place you must have a licence.

For information contact:

Performer Rights Society
29–33 Berners Street
London W1P 4AA.

Self Assessments and Activities

1 Find out the requirements of your local authority for setting up a beauty salon.

2 Design a salon layout for a room 9 m × 5 m to include a changing cubicle area and reception area. Consider:

   (a) colour scheme/decor;

   (b) flooring;

   (c) lighting;

   (d) equipment/furniture.

3 Make a list of the essential equipment you would need if you were working alone in a small salon. Cost the equipment by writing to manufacturers/wholesalers for estimates.

4 Draw the salon layout and label the size of the treatment room(s) in your college or work experience placement and discuss whether or not you would like to make any changes.

5 Design and cost the layout of a beauty room 7 m × 7 m. The room has a small window and you will need to consider decor, flooring, heating, lighting, equipment etc.

CHAPTER 16

Running your salon – Products and services

OBJECTIVES

This chapter explains the various aspects of running your salon. It considers buying stock and the advantages and disadvantages of buying products from wholesalers, manufacturers and cash and carry wholesalers. Your product range, how to select a product and the advantages of producing 'own-brand' products are covered. The services you offer your clients will be largely dependent on the skills of your staff.

The daily operating requirements of your salon revolve around cash handling, security, banking, cleaning and laundry and salon maintenance, work schedules and rotas. Costing and being cost effective are important and must be taken into account at the initial planning stage. The salon owner must also be aware of certain legislation as laid down in the Consumer Protection Act 1987, Supply of Goods and Services Act 1994, Resale Prices Acts 1964 and 1976 and Trade Descriptions Acts 1968 and 1972.

BUYING STOCK

Stock can be bought from:

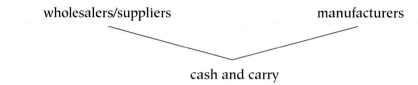

wholesalers/suppliers   manufacturers

cash and carry
wholesalers

Wholesalers/suppliers advantages:

- sell a wide range of products;
- often, there is no minimum order;
- may offer monthly terms (30 days' credit);
- will deliver your materials.

Cash and carry wholesalers advantages:

- allow you to buy what you want when you want it; *but*

Cash and carry wholesalers disadvantages:

- you may be tempted to buy more because of product display;
- you have to go and buy it.

Manufacturers send out representatives and they only sell their own company products. They might offer:

- sales literature;
- up-to-date information with their products;
- demonstrations in your salon (usually free of charge);
- a minimum order value;
- training with their products;
- a credit period (30 days).

There are a number of points to consider when you buy stock. A credit period can assist your cash flow, and 'buying as you go along' can be useful when you are budgeting.

> Consider the benefits then decide on the best method for you.

SELECTING YOUR PRODUCT RANGE

This is a very important area to consider. It needs time and patience. You may be fortunate to have worked with a professional range of products and already decided that you will use that range. If not, what must you consider?

Figure 16.1 Cash and carry wholesale facilities

Most products have **a selling life span**. The new product is:

introduced → its demand grows

|

its demand matures

|

its demand declines

Some products will sell longer than others but, eventually, manufacturers of a successful range of products will feel that the range must be:

- re-energised, and so the range is increased.

This means that:

- old products are faded out; and
- new ones take their place.

There are advantages and disadvantages to this, but manufacturers know their work. They can:

- offer you an **efficient service**; and
- **meet your needs**.

You will need to look around and **investigate the market**. This would be a good time to complete a SWOT analysis (see page 76) and see the products that are already in the immediate area. Consider:

The **cost to you** of salon products.

The **cost to your clients** of retail products.

Your profit margin.

The Features and Benefits (FAB) of the products

The more expensive the product, the greater your profit margin will be. Make sure:

your products are client affordable.

LAUNCH PACKS – OPENING ORDER

One company offers a full information package to prospective stockists outlining:

- the need for professional products;
- the cost;
- the retailing profitability (what it means for you);
- the cost of treatments using the product;
- considering competitors.

This is essential starter information.

If the salon responds:

- a New Business Consultant will visit the premises and provide on-site advice and check the salon's suitability;
- a tailor-made opening order is then discussed.

For around £2000 + VAT a salon could receive:

- 1 week intensive product training;
- free on-going training in skincare with products for staff and a technical manual;
- a full range of professional salon products;
- a full range of retail products;
- an extensive range of salon support material
  - product samples
  - display material
  - consultation cards
  - prescription cards
  - fact sheets/brochures
  - stock sheets to assist monitoring and re-ordering
  - all the above material free-of-charge with on-going orders
- no re-ordering restrictions free p+p on orders over £250.00;
- promotional events/evening. A demonstrator will support salon events for individuals or groups and supply relevant materials;
- marketing plan – this can be formatted to meet the individual salon's requirements with the company;
- the company will provide 20% discount on all educational training courses that operate through their Group Institute;
- Salon Awards:
  - A variety of opportunities to participate in: **Skin Care Centre of the Year Highest Achiever**.

Opening packages come with a price tag, sometimes a large one. Always check if it's negotiable and that it is tailor-made to your needs.

There are plenty of product companies.

Make sure that you obtain lots of:
- information;
- free advice;
- demonstrations;

before you decide to select a product.

You may prefer to use one of the professional mail order stockists.

This means that:
- you order only what you want;
- there is no minimum order;
- depending on how much your order is you can receive up to 50% discount on promotional literature and samples;
- you can receive loyalty vouchers.

You must buy:
- your technical training manual;
- self-training videos;
- promotional materials;
- samples.

You will need to consider the needs of:
- your business;
- your staff;
- your clients;

and decide which product stockist best meets your requirements.

PRODUCING YOUR 'OWN-BRAND' PRODUCTS

This can be prestigious for you if you find a good company that produces 'own-brand' products, and you like the quality of the product. Own-brand products mean:
- you have a professional identity;
- you will have a higher profit margin;
- a good reason for selling.

If you decide to consider this scheme, you will need to test some product ranges first to make sure they meet your needs. **Own-brand products** can be found in **trade journals** and at **trade shows and exhibitions**.

 REMEMBER: make sure you insure adequately for product liability. See Chapter 9.

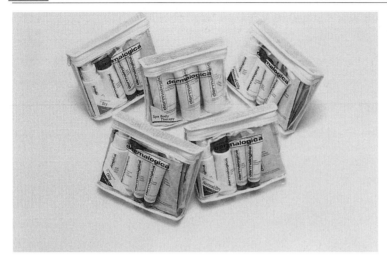

Figure 16.2 A product display

WHAT TREATMENTS WILL YOU OFFER?

This will depend on the skills of your staff. Beauty therapists who hold full recognised diplomas will be able to offer all the general treatments. In addition, you may have wisely recruited staff with additional skills such as:

- reflexology;
- micro-lifting;
- aromatherapy;
- permanent pigmentation;
- ear piercing;
- acrylic nails;
- sports therapy.

You will want to consider your range of services with the staff and equipment you have available.

DAILY REQUIREMENTS

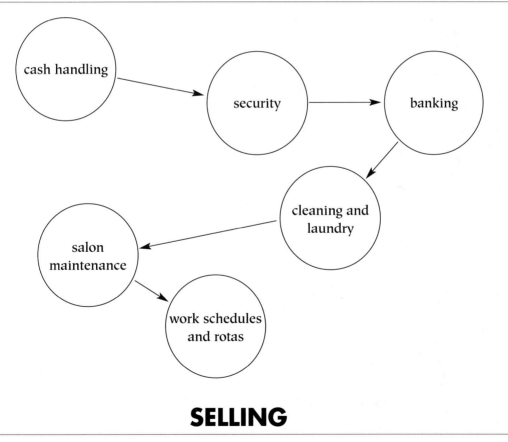

SELLING

You will probably have a system to record your staff's sales and if not it will be necessary for you to create one. This will help you to:

- monitor the individual therapist's sales;
- calculate commission;
- consider sales techniques in the therapist's appraisal.

In order to sell effectively the client has got to want the product or service. The client must feel that the service or product is right for him or her.

Knowledgeable staff:
- know their products
- know their services
- can calculate what a client needs (see page 64).

SALON SECURITY

An electronic **cash register** will satisfy many needs. It is:
- secure;
- helps accuracy;
- will show daily income;
- can record and print other information (depending on the model).

If money is kept at the salon it **should be secure in a cash register** or in a safe. Banking should be done as often as possible for **safe** handling of money. Your **local crime prevention officer** will advise you on **salon security**, such as burglar alarms. These alarms can be linked to the security provider or the police and gives a quick response to burglary. The salon should also be fitted with security locks for doors and windows.

Your salon should be cleaned at least once a day and regular attention paid to any untidiness as it occurs. Everyone is responsible for a clean, safe establishment.

> Good organisation is vital

CLEANING, LAUNDRY AND MAINTENANCE

Washing towels and gowns is a regular daily feature. Your *own* laundry service is the most efficient method for maintaining regular supplies, so invest in a good washing machine and tumble dryer.

Just as your salon needs cleaning, it will need to have regular maintenance to maintain high standards for health and safety. Make sure you find a reliable maintenance person. This will be an asset.

These could be **daily** occurrences in the salon. *Don't wait* until they happen to find a person to fix them.

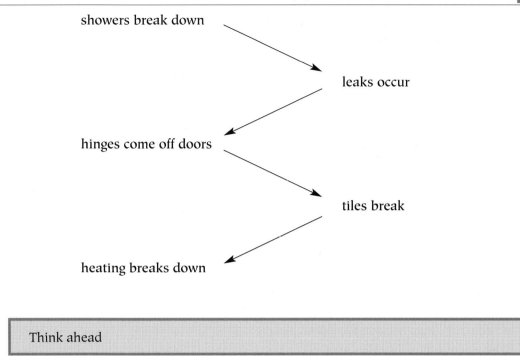

showers break down

leaks occur

hinges come off doors

tiles break

heating breaks down

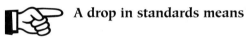

Think ahead

A drop in standards means

a drop in business

Failure to carry out essential repairs means that you could be reported to the Environmental Health and your business could be at risk.

Checking and maintaining work schedules and rotas

You will be responsible for creating a staff work rota to ensure that the business is properly operative at all times.

In order for your rota to be effective you will need to consider various points:
- the hours the salon is open;
- evening shifts;
- Saturdays;
- the number of staff;
- maximum staff coverage on busy days.

You may have a **fixed** weekly rota or a more flexible two- or three-weekly rota.

In order for staff to be satisfied you will need to consider:
- how many late shifts;
- how many Saturdays;

they will work.

Once the rota is established it should be **monitored** to check its suitability. It should be flexible enough to allow staff to swap shifts if necessary.

A flexible rota enables staff to plan ahead and have a different day off each week if they wish.

Planning work schedules

Staff will need to have a list of duties or a work schedule so that they know what their responsibilities are in the business.

They will need a schedule that shows:
- daily tasks;
- areas of responsibility.

These should be clearly stated and displayed in the business so that staff can refer to them.

Careful monitoring is required to ensure that:
- all tasks are covered;
- new ones may be added when necessary;
- staff are completing the tasks;
- the selected tasks ensure the smooth running of the business.

Self Assessments and Activities

1 Plan a fixed rota for four beauty therapists in a salon that opens 10.00 a.m.–6.00 p.m. Monday, Tuesday, Wednesday and Saturday, 10.00 a.m.–9.00 p.m. Thursday and Friday.

2 Plan a flexible rota for the salon described.

3 Plan a work schedule for three beauty therapists showing their daily tasks and responsibilities.

CLIENT RECORDS

Wherever you decide to keep your client information:
- on a computer (see page 94, Data Protection Act);
- in a filing box; or
- in a filing cabinet;

ensure that it is never on public display, for example, a record card left on the reception desk. This information is private and confidential and is necessary only for the therapist to perform the best treatments.

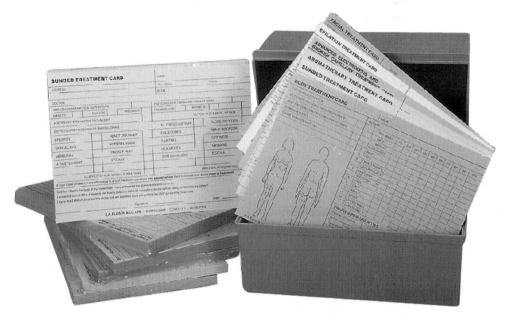

Figure 16.3 Record systems

  REMEMBER leave a file, lose a client.

Confidentiality and professionalism are necessary at all times and reflect **your** standards and the standards in **your** salon.

BEING 'COST' EFFECTIVE

If you are retailing a particular range of products, the manufacturer will have given you a suggested retail price (SRP). It is a guideline only and you are allowed to charge more or less than the SRP.

Products and materials that you use in the salon will be 'costed' by calculating expenditure and time for the services you offer. **Costing** is calculated by **taking the hourly (monthly) rate for each member of staff and adding your proportional costs to it**. You will then:

- calculate the total sum; and
- divide it by the number of working weeks.

This figure will give you the basic amount that must be earned per hour. You must then add your profit.

Calculate all your expenses to find what you must earn per hour. Then you will be **cost effective** in your salon.

CONSUMER PROTECTION ACT 1987 AND THE COSMETICS PRODUCTS REGULATIONS 1989

There are a number of Acts which the salon owner must be aware of that relate to the products that are used and sold. The **Consumer Protection Act 1987** aims to safeguard the consumer from products that do not reach a reasonable level of safety. This is particularly important in the salon because of product liability. Part I of the Act deals with product liability.

In the past, injured persons had to prove a manufacturer negligent before they could sue for damages. This Act removes the need to prove negligence. The Act implements the EC directive on product liability, which provides a similar degree of protection for people in the EC.

An injured person can take action against:

producers
|
importers
|
own-branders

Other suppliers, such as wholesalers and retailers, are not liable unless they fail to identify the producer or own-brander if asked to do so by the injured person.

Liability under this Act is not restricted to consumer goods. Goods used at a place of work are included as well as components and raw materials of a product.

Detailed information on this Act can be obtained from:
Consumer Safety Unit
Department of Trade and Industry
1 Victoria Street
London SW1H 0ET

THE SALE AND SUPPLY OF GOODS ACT 1994

This Act replaced the Sale of Goods and Services Act 1982.

This act deals with consumers' rights and traders' obligations in relation to **goods** and **services**.

Goods
- as part of a service;
- on hire;
- in part-exchange.

This Act stipulates that the goods supplied must be:

- of 'merchantable' quality (satisfactory);
- fit for the particular purpose that the supplier seller claims they are;
- fit the description given.

Services

A person providing a service must give the service

- with reasonable care and skill;
- within a reasonable time;
- for a reasonable price.

TRADE DESCRIPTIONS ACT 1968–1972

This Act is concerned with the **false description of goods**. It is a crime to mislead the public. The Law says that the retailer must not:

- supply misleading information;
- falsely describe or make false statements about products or services.

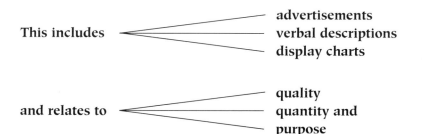

This includes
- advertisements
- verbal descriptions
- display charts

and relates to
- quality
- quantity and
- purpose

The retailer must:

- not make false comparisons between present and former prices;
- not offer products at half-price unless they have already been offered at the actual price for at least twenty-eight days;
- be aware of statements saying that something is 'our price' and it is worth 'double the amount';
- be aware that price comparisons are misleading and can be illegal.

The Trades Description Act 1972 stipulates that products must be labelled with the country of origin.

RE-SALE PRICES ACTS 1964 AND 1976

These Acts stipulate that manufacturers and wholesalers cannot compel retailers to sell their goods at a fixed price. They can suggest recommended suitable prices.

Suppliers cannot withhold stock from retailers who choose to sell below the suggested price. One exception is that: suppliers can set a price if it is 'in the public interest'.

Interview with Gina – beauty salon manager in a health spa

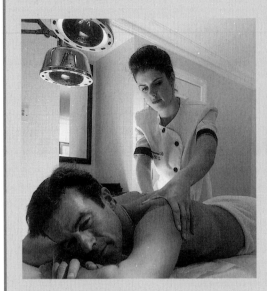

Gina works in a beauty salon in a large spa, in a prestigious four star hotel in Runnymede, near Windsor, Berkshire.

The spa is spacious and creates a calm relaxed atmosphere. There is a large reception area from which the vast neo-classical swimming pool and whirlpool can be viewed. There is also a steam and sauna bath, beauty centre and gymnasium.

The treatment rooms can be reached from the reception area and are adjacent to the Hair Studio. The Garden Room provides light lunches and refreshment and there is a supervised gym, dance studio and snooker room.

Gina has worked at the Spa for just two months and already has a number of plans for the Beauty Centre.

Q: How did you start your career in Beauty Therapy?
I lived in Devon and went to college when I left school. I studied Beauty Therapy at Exeter College and completed a two year course and gained a Diploma from City and Guilds and IHBC. I also trained in Sports Therapy.

Whilst studying for a BTEC European Studies Diploma (a one year course), I went to work in Rennes in Brittany, France. I worked in a large, busy salon and gained considerable experience. I was also able to go to University for three months to improve my French.

Q: Where did you go from there?

I went to work at Ragdale Hall Health Hydro, Leicestershire. I enjoyed the variety and challenge of the work in the Hydro. I assisted in the in-house training of junior therapists and enjoyed sales promotions, demonstrations evenings.

After four years I wanted to progress and by chance, through a friend, I heard of a Beauty Therapist Manager's position at Pine Trees Health and Leisure, Leicester. A busy place in the town centre. I was successful and I was now on a managerial salary with commission and manager perks, such as freebies and promotions from the Cosmetic Houses.

Q: Tell me about your work there

The Leisure Complex had over 2000 members and I worked as **part of a management team**. We worked well together and **team spirit** was very important. There was a lot of training in Sales, Business Plans and Accounts and this developed my management skills.

I still worked five days a week on beauty treatments and had to fit administrative work around clients. I often worked a seven day week because as a manager you always have to stand in or be prepared to work if it's necessary.

I believe you must be **dedicated** to your work. I'm also very **enthusiastic** about what I do and I like to enjoy my working situation.

Q: Do you enjoy training?

Yes, as part of the work. I like sales and promotions and it's important for therapists to learn to do this as well. I've always worked to **targets** and therapists that don't meet their targets need help by training. This helps the therapist to develop her **confidence** as well as achieving her targets and earning commission. Most therapists work on a basic salary and commission so it's an essential part of work.

Q: Are there any particular methods you use for promotions?

I like to make follow up telephone calls to clients that haven't been for a treatment for a long while. A courtesy telephone call does usually remind the client to re-book and offers an opportunity to promote the latest product or offer. Most clients re-book immediately and appreciate a call.

Q: Why did you leave Pine Trees Leisure?

I wanted more of a challenge. I set **personal goals** for each position that I'm in and I'd reached these. I was still doing five full days of treatments and I wanted more management. I believe it is vital to keep doing treatments but as a stand-in/cover or for training.

I thought of going overseas again, so I contacted 'Beauty Connections' Agency in London, but they came up with this position at the Runnymede and I thought it would be a great opportunity. I have five full time therapists and soon two part time therapists and an osteopath for three days a week and one Alternative Treatments Therapist for Reiki and Hopi ear candles. There are seven treatment rooms and the hydro-room. The therapists have a uniform and shoes provided and must wear hair up to conform to professional codes, a minimum of jewellery is also allowed. The Spa and Beauty Reception have four full-time staff and four part-time staff. They have their own manager. I liaise with her and offer training in 'types of treatment' to ensure that the receptionists understand the treatments and the time that must be allowed when booking-in clients.

The Beauty Centre is open 10.00–8.00/9.00 p.m. on weekdays and 10.00–6.00 p.m. at weekends. The hotel guests use the Spa and do have treatments, but mainly at weekends.

Q: Tell me about your clientele?

We have 1350 Spa members and a number of these use the beauty facilities, but we also have a lot of local trade, non-Spa members. I think they like a luxurious place to come to even if they do not require membership of the rest of the Spa. We offer a variety of packages for individuals or small groups, for example:
A 'Pamper Day' costing   £105.00 Mon–Fri   £120. Sat–Sun
may consist of a prescription facial, a therapeutic full body massage and a manicure.

Clients can also use Spa facilities and enjoy a Spa lunch in the Garden Room. The Beauty Centre is booked most of the time, and so is the Hair Studio. The Hair Studio is a franchise and run by two business partners, but we cross promote and this is good for both businesses.

Q: What is your job description?

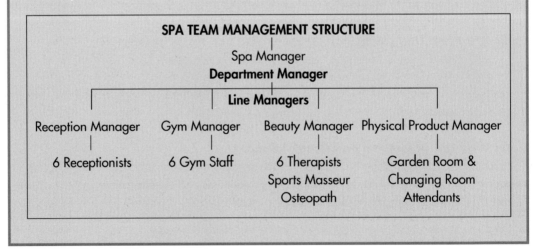

SPA TEAM MANAGEMENT STRUCTURE

Spa Manager
Department Manager

Line Managers

Reception Manager	Gym Manager	Beauty Manager	Physical Product Manager
6 Receptionists	6 Gym Staff	6 Therapists Sports Masseur Osteopath	Garden Room & Changing Room Attendants

I am Beauty Manager of the Centre and part-time Duty Manager for the Spa, which means in addition to running the Beauty I also take shifts as Duty Manager which involves mainly **client care** more than the physical Spa problems, although naturally I would have to deal with these if they were an issue and also the smooth running of the Spa. So being trained in Sports Therapy is an asset as well as being able to fetch and carry towels! I wear a uniform of navy jacket, skirt and shoes and a white blouse. My Rota varies, but this week it is:

M.	6–2 p.m.	Duty and Beauty Manager
T.	10–6 p.m.	Beauty Manager
W.	10–6 p.m.	Beauty Manager
T.	6–2 p.m.	Duty and Beauty Manager
F.	2–10 p.m.	Duty and Beauty Manager
S.	Off	In on Saturday
S.	Off	

I should be off but we have a therapist sick so I shall be working. This is routine. My work involves all the Beauty Centre Management which means:

- effective running of the Centre – planning, staff and organisation;
- stock control – buying
- staff management/recruitment/rotas
- preparation of wages/commission to be submitted on computer to Hotel Accounts;
- staff training – in house, external;
- I attend weekly Duty Manager meetings;
- I hold **staff meetings** every three to four weeks unless there's a problem. I communicate mainly through memos on a daily basis;
- I am responsible for all client records (on computer) and for day files for day clients;
- I show round potential clients/members to see the entire facilities. I believe this is very important;
- **advertising/marketing**, I would liaise with the Hotel Marketing Department. This is not required at this time;
- **research** into new treatments:
  I book into salons to have treatments and assess the treatment, then check out where it is given throughout the country;
- appraisals – 6 monthly. The Hotel is very keen on this. It should be informal but after the **appraiser** has carried out intensive research on the **appraisee**. This is a good opportunity to note **training needs** or to follow up if training has been given, although the therapist doesn't have to wait for an appraisal to state training needs. Anyone can say informally at any time what they want to do and I must act on this. This is good because I can identify the **needs**.

Q: What type of in-house training is on offer?
Customer Care The Hotel are very keen on this as they are **Investors in People** and

feel it is vital to good business. I am also a big believer in client care so this is always on-going.
First Aid
Management Skills
Computer Training
and any area that one wants to improve on.

Q: Are all your Beauty Therapists qualified in Beauty Therapy and Electrology?
Yes, but it is becoming necessary for therapists to be **aromatherapists** and **reflexologists** as well so I will be considering external college courses for some of them. We do train in communication skills and personal skills but maturity is another matter and must be considered for certain clientele. We train also in particular methods that are required for specialist product treatments. This is very important because it affects both treatments and sales.

I set the **Sales Targets** and the therapists work on basic pay and commission. The product houses also offer **incentives** so these are solid reasons to improve personal sales figures.

Q: Do the staff have any perks?
The staff have the use of the Spa facilities and the opportunity to do treatments on each other, but there is seldom time for this.

Q: So what are your plans for the Centre?
I'm very keen to get the therapists involved in **Salon of the Year** and **Therapist of the Year**. I want to establish a good **team spirit/team worker** and build strong relationships. This is the Business Plan for success. I am a self-motivator and believe that **motivation** is vital if businesses are to be progressive, so personal motivation enhances the working environment. Everyone needs a **challenge** and reward so **effective treatments** and **after sales** carried out by **competent caring staff** who work well together and are **effective communicators** with their clients are the basis of a good business.

I'm really looking forward to working with the staff to develop the Centre. I feel that I have settled in and already we are working well together as a team.

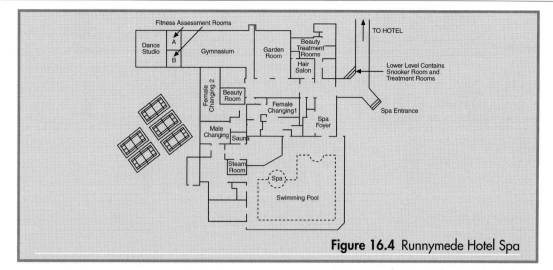

Figure 16.4 Runnymede Hotel Spa

Self Assessments and Activities

1 Design a business card and letter heading for a small salon and an attractive leaflet with your price list. Find out the cost of printing this material. Obtain at least two quotations.

2 Write to two product companies and find out what they would offer you in a launch pack if you were setting up in business.

3 Make a list of all the daily requirements that you might have to check if you were a salon owner.

4 A knowledge of the Consumer Protection Act 1987 is vital if you are a salon owner. Make a list of the reasons why you think this to be so.

5 Explain the importance of the Trade Descriptions Acts 1968 and 1972 to a retailer.

6 Explain the factors that should be taken into account when selecting a product range.

7 In small groups, research

   a) the Consumer Protection Act 1987;

   b) the Supply of Goods and Services 1994;

   and state your responsibilities as a salon owner.

8 Investigate 2 product ranges. Consider:
   • the cost;
   • quality;
   • packaging;
   • salon/client benefit.

9 Plan a work schedule for 4 beauty therapists showing their daily tasks and responsibilities.

10 Create a check list for your staff to ensure that salon security checks are made at the beginning and end of the working day.

CHAPTER 17

Marketing and promotion

OBJECTIVES

This chapter deals with marketing – providing your clients with the services and products they need. You may use market research to assess their needs.

There are many forms of promotions you may choose – advertising, mail-shots, leaflets, newspapers, national directories, demonstrations, bridal fayres, video and window displays for example.

A computer could be a useful business aid and could assist you in producing promotional literature, controlling stock, financial forecasting and storing information about clients. You may need to register with the Data Protection Registrar if you store clients' personal details on your computer (see page 94).

Marketing is about supplying your clients with the services and products they need. It is not just selling services and products to people. It usually means that you have **considered the needs** of the **consumer** in your immediate area.

You will have already organised some **market research** to be sure you have a market for your business. Your **marketing philosophy** is based on having:

goods services/products
|
at the right price
|
in the right place
|
at the right time

Effective promotions means you have conveyed the above to the consumer and she will want to come to your salon.

Marketing is a continual process. You will need to ensure that you **monitor** your clients needs all the time.

Do you
- have a wide age-range of clients;
- sell a full-range of treatments;
- sell a full product range to match your treatments/age range?

If you answer **No** to any of these questions then you must decide how to increase your market. By careful analysis you must decide on the best method to promote your sales/service. Market client research.

Listen to your clients, ask their advice
- on your services or any new services;
- your products.

Clients enjoy participating, especially if they benefit from the outcomes. Make it a regular feature.

Questionnaires are a useful form of analysis and self-assessment. They should be completed after demonstrations and open day events.

 REMEMBER

client assessment
|
means self-assessment
|
self-improvement
|
salon success

Promotions are necessary if the public are to know that your salon exists.

Today there is so much choice available to the prospective client that you must ensure that she selects your salon. There are many forms of promotion. Advertising is one.

ADVERTISING

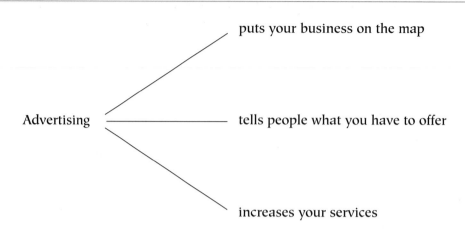

There are many forms of advertising. You will have to decide which form is best for your needs.

After using various methods it is important to monitor the success of your advertising. You must ensure that you keep a record of how new clients come to your salon. Product sales should increase after promotions, if not, why not? You need to **evaluate the outcomes**.

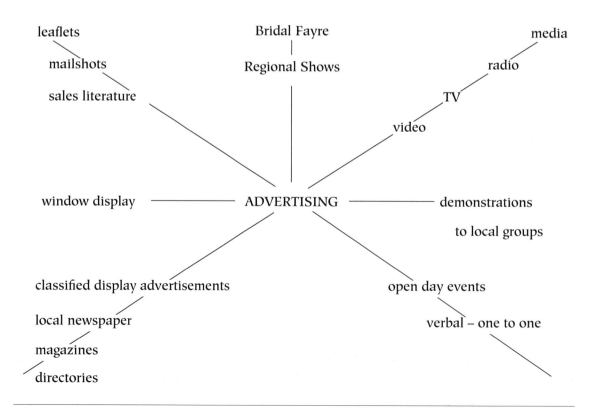

Classified and display advertising

Regular classified advertisements in a local paper can be advantageous and not too expensive, and you may be able to have a feature on your salon or your products in a local paper. You may be able to contribute to the paper.

Display advertising can be expensive.

National directories

Directories can be very helpful to a business. Local (regional) Directories can offer free advice on advertising and inclusion of your salon's name and address and telephone number in the directory can be inexpensive.

National Directories such as **Yellow Pages** will cost more but have national circulation. You must decide what would be more profitable for you.

Open-days/evenings

Open-days should be a regular feature in a salon. It's a good opportunity to invite existing clients and they can bring a friend which introduces them to you and your business. You could extend the invitation to the general public or you could alternate your open-days sometimes inviting a restricted clientele.

This makes

people feel special
offers are exclusively for them
it gives a sense of identity with the salon
an evening out

Clients will often book treatments and buy products. This is the time to

demonstrate new treatments
launch a new product and show existing ones

You will probably provide a buffet and refreshment but you will need the facilities to offer this separately as you do not want food and drink in the sales area. It is a good idea for staff to drink and eat after the event. This means they are not munching and talking to people at the same time.

 REMEMBER
Be professional at all times

Clients can be given many incentives

special offers on treatments
freebies
your product company will probably send a representative
and provide promotional material (see page 148).

Most of all the event gives the clients the opportunity to have a greater identity with your salon.

For the newcomer it is a 'way-in' to your establishment and an opportunity to get to know staff before having a treatment.

Media/local radio

This is a good way to reach a wide range of people. Get to know your local station – offer a service e.g. seasonal health and beauty tips can be popular. You might be offered a regular space.

Video advertising

This is frequently seen in Hospitals, Health Centres, Shopping Malls. It can be expensive but it reaches a lot of people. It could be a good option or you could have your own unit.

A video unit

This can promote products and services by displaying the sequence of specialised treatments and you can make your own videos.

You will need to:
- change the material regularly;
- have 'touch control' for individual operating so it is not running all the time;
- consider its position carefully.

Leaflets

If you own a computer, a local leaflet drop can be quite inexpensive, and can be a useful way of telling people about your services. A **special offer** or **voucher** attached to this can be an added incentive for the prospective client. However, if you use this method make sure you limit the time that the voucher is valid.

Mailshots

These can also be produced quite simply and professionally on your personal computer (more costly if you have to have them printed). However, postage can be expensive. This could be a **good promotional opportunity** every few months with existing clients and their friends. You could:
- offer a 'freebie' treatment or product;
- offer a reduced price;
- offer a voucher;
- promote a new service;
- promote a seasonal product;
- promote an existing service.

Demonstrations to local groups

Local groups, for example the women's guild, charity groups and church groups, are always wanting speakers or demonstrators. Most salon owners would use this opportunity to:

- meet prospective clients;
- show the services they can offer;
- distribute promotional literature;
- exercise good public relations.

It is an excellent way to meet people, **talk to them** and **invite them to your salon**. This gives you the opportunity to:

- promote your image; and
- sell your professional expertise.

There is usually a lot of interest in a demonstration with lots of questions to be answered. Make sure you have the time to talk to people.

 REMEMBER first impressions count.

Stay calm and reflect the professional person. No amount of advertising can make up for the **personal touch**. If you consider large-scale demonstrations:

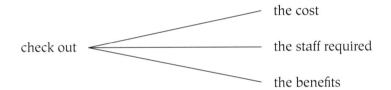

check out
- the cost
- the staff required
- the benefits

If you have staff who are confident demonstrators and the cost to you is not too high and the benefits are good, then this is a good form of promotion.

Quite often these events can be costly and the return is small – another form of advertising may suit your needs better.

Make-up demonstrations are always popular and you will probably offer a home-visiting wedding service. This can also be a good way of promoting your salon as it allows you to meet many prospective clients. **Dress shops** and **bridal shops** are good places to leave leaflets and your business cards.

A bridal package is often used by **advertisers** to take the strain out of wedding preparations. You might participate in:

- a local advertisement, selling space with printers, hotels, etc;
- join with a bridal shop in advertising.

This can be very productive if your salon is in a busy area and developing good business relationships generates new business. Everyone can benefit.

BRIDAL FAYRES

These are held by companies such as 'Starting Together' who produce a local Wedding Guide Booklet (Regional) which combine the main services required for a wedding. The Booklet allows you **to advertise your service** and/or you can pay to have a stall at the Fayre which is held at a large hotel in the area. The stall allows you to demonstrate your services and discuss your particular **Wedding Package**: e.g. bride make-up, bridesmaids and mother of the bride.

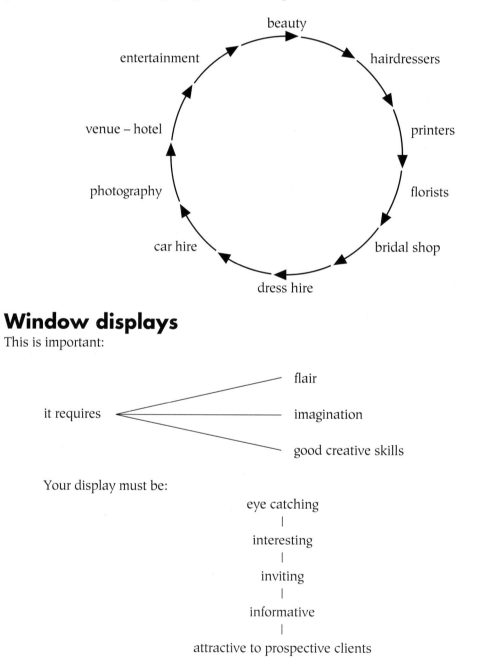

Window displays

This is important:

it requires
- flair
- imagination
- good creative skills

Your display must be:

eye catching
|
interesting
|
inviting
|
informative
|
attractive to prospective clients

It will not do this if it is:

crowded
|
dull
|
stale

Promotional literature and display material can obtained from suppliers:

> Always obtain it, use it and change it regularly.

Window displays changed regularly look as good as when you first displayed them. A display should never be left until it looks stale. All product material must be 'dummies' to ensure
- health and safety;
- no mess;
- excellent appearance.

Check you have sufficient display board and cabinets to make the display effective. Your finished display should **achieve your aim** i.e. to promote your product.

Evaluate your project
- Is it well balanced and eye catching?
- Is it fresh, clean, creative?
- Is the lighting correct?
- Has your theme been successfully communicated?
- Is it safe and secure?

If you cannot produce a good window display, find someone who can! **Plan your** promotions and advertising on a yearly basis:

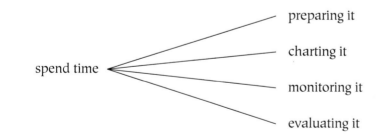

spend time
- preparing it
- charting it
- monitoring it
- evaluating it

Keep within your budget.

Self Assessments and Activities

1 Prepare a questionnaire in order to carry out market research in your area, on the type of people that use beauty salons and the treatments they prefer.

2 Design some promotional material for your salon.

3 Design a leaflet for a housedrop to encourage new business.

4 Obtain details on the Data Protection Act and list how it affects the salon owner who stores personal details about clients on a computer.

5 Contact your local newspaper and find out how much a small classified advertisement would cost.

6 How much would display advertising cost – consider two examples.

7 What advantages would display advertising offer you?

8 Design a salon price list for a trendy high street salon.

9 Design a 'homecare' leaflet for an Epilation client.

10 Write a small feature for your local newspaper beauty page, promoting one seasonal treatment (e.g. waxing).

11 Plan the Grand Opening of your new salon.

12 a) Prepare a talk to give to a woman's group on facial therapy or aromatherapy

   b) With a colleague practise the talk and get her to make a video

   c) Carry out some self-assessment and consider how you might improve the talk e.g. body language

   d) Your colleague could carry out some peer assessment by evaluating your talk.

13 Prepare a promotion for a product as a display for reception or the salon window.

   a) List your requirements

   b) Plan your promotion

   c) Display and photograph your work

Interview with Suzanne – sole trader/mobile therapist
Q: Tell me how your career in Beauty Therapy started?

When I left school I trained as a secretary, I worked for various companies for eight years. I never really liked the work but it was an income. I had a good social life and two horses to upkeep and a career wasn't my main priority.

At 24 I felt I'd reached maturity and suddenly I thought I'm working five days a week and I'm bored out of my mind. I realised that I wanted to do something I enjoyed. I wanted to be more focused and train for a profession, I wished I'd trained sooner rather than later.

I was interested in Beauty and started an evening class for Personal Beauty Care. This was at a local college, Langley, East Berkshire. I was so impressed with the facilities and the professionalism of the staff I thought I wanted to do more. I also wanted to pursue a career that I could continue if I had children.

I discussed it with my partner and he supported me for the next eighteen months while I trained as a Beauty Therapist. I qualified through the ITEC Examination System. After eighteen months I studied Electrical Epilation, Aromatherapy and Reflexology as part-time evening courses.

Q: How did you start working?
I wanted full-time work so I went to a Health and Beauty Recruitment Agency in Covent Garden. I did a **trade test** at the agency, a sample of my skills, and gained part-time employment at Champneys Health Resort. It was a very good experience offering a full range of treatments, and it was very busy.

Q: When did you leave?
After seven months I felt I could work well on my own. I looked for a place that I could establish myself. I already had a portable couch and some portable equipment which I'd bought gradually throughout my training.

I found a hairdressers in Ealing, London. The salon owner was keen for me to develop a beauty therapy business and had a room that was ideal. He wanted me to be an employee. I agreed to this because it meant that he funded the business and I had a free range in setting up the room. I also developed an evening mobile practice in Surrey where I lived because I'd had a number of enquiries through friends and it seemed silly to miss the opportunity.

I enjoyed the challenge of starting and developing the business, but I found the salon owner had no knowledge of Beauty Therapy and it made advertising difficult because he wasn't really aware of the needs and I wasn't free to advertise as I wanted.

Q: What about your clientele?
They were very mixed. The area had a number of salons and a lot of clients were passing trade which made it difficult to build a therapist/client relationship. I had to work hard at advertising because of the competition. I used local newspaper advertisements and vouchers but I found an 'A' Board outside the hairdressers one of the best forms of advertising.

Q: What made you leave the salon?
Well, I found I'd gained enough experience to go it alone and being mobile as well I enjoyed the flexibility and being in control. So I decided to look for a room to rent, but locally in Surrey. I wanted to continue with my mobile work but have a base as well and it seemed more sensible to work in the same area.

I found a small hairdressing salon with just two members of staff, including the owner. It had a large, bright suitable room, which had previously been used for Beauty Therapy but had not developed to its full potential. It already had local authority approval but I had to be re-inspected when I was there.

The owner wanted 30% of my takings for rent which included the receptionists duties so appointments were taken care of. I thought that this was very fair because it would help when income was low.

The room had a trolley, magnifying lamp and adequate lighting and it was pleasantly decorated in pink.

Q: How did you finance the business and did you find it easy to get established?

My mobile work funded the business and the outlay was quite small apart from advertising and I certainly gained knowledge after being in the other salon, although this one was different. I had very little to buy as I already owned portable equipment. It's situated in the High Street of a small village. The area is affluent and the people are middle-aged, 90% of the trade is local.

When I started to establish myself, I wanted to really condense the advertising to keep the cost down. I decided to go for a desk top publishing and have a really good master leaflet prepared in Black and White. This was expensive initially but would save money later. After I could photocopy any number but the quality would always be there.

I chose to put the price list, my details and the appointment 'card' all on one leaflet. This works very well because clients tend to keep it because it has the appointment on it. It also means that I don't need a separate business card.

Initially I did a leaflet drop and put them in the local shops. Gradually I had a gentle stream of clients who returned and became regulars. Now I tend to find clients come because friends have recommended them. I haven't really found a need for any other promotions. Good client communication and good service has been my best advertisement.

Q: How often do you work there?

At the moment I'm happy with 50–50. I still enjoy mobile but it's good having a base. I usually work two full days 9.00 a.m.–7.00 p.m. and half-a-day.

Q: What about your products and retail products?

I feel that it is important to have stock that turns over quickly. So I buy a range that has no minimum order and I don't need to hold too much stock.

I suppose my retail outlet is small. I sell to complement my work so I feel that I offer a service that also helps my clients and assists my work with homecare. It seems fine at the moment.

Q: Do you have any plans?
Not yet, I'm still enjoying this set-up. I like being a sole-trader. I enjoy being in control. I do my own accounts on a daily basis and submit them to the Inland Revenue at the end of the tax year. I have variety in my work by having the salon and being mobile and I enjoy the flexibility and the freedom – I have a life! I still keep horses and enjoy riding. If I had a larger business I think that I would have to be more committed and then I would lose some of my leisure time.

I certainly enjoy this situation when I worked at the Health Hydro I felt it was very claustrophobic working in cubicles and very pressurised. I also spent a lot of time travelling. My present work style provides me with a reasonable income and allows me leisure time, which is very important to me.

Q: Are there any disadvantages?
Well obviously if you don't work you have no income and insurance for this is very expensive. I think that this is the only one that affects me. I could save on a regular basis to try and overcome this problem if it arises. Holidays are not a problem. I tend to take short breaks and book clients around them.

At the moment I am confident that I am developing a sound business in mobile and salon and as I like the two situations I have no plans to expand, just to make an effective business.

CHAPTER 18

Business cycles

OBJECTIVES

The salon owner must be aware of the changing **Business Cycles** as this means the business has to adapt accordingly. All businesses experience the primary cycle, growth, maturity and sometimes saturation but not always decline. Recession is another business stage.

Recession means that there is little or no growth in industry on a national scale. The country's lack of prosperity is reflected in a drop in consumer spending.

The salon owner must be inventive and resourceful and use all her skills during a recession in order to adapt and create business. Adapting to survive is part of business and bankruptcy should not occur if you have taken note of financial forecasting and acted accordingly. Preventative measures in the early stages of recession assist the future.

A business will fluctuate in performance, but it is essential for the business to adjust to the different business cycles. Business **forecasts** (cash flow forecasts) will enable you to draw up forecast charts that ensure you anticipate the quieter times and plan for them.

Initially your business is in a **Primary Cycle**. You are gaining many new clients and you establish a retail trade. Satisfied clients return to your salon regularly and you are still gaining new clients. The **Growth Cycle** is developing steadily or rapidly depending on your business expertise and your business continues to expand. A thriving business works hard to maintain the **growth cycle** but the salon owner must always be aware of changes in the environment, the market place i.e.

- competition – a new salon;
- local/national unemployment;

which could affect trade and growth.

The **Maturity Cycle** is when a business is established and can manage to maintain growth even with competitors. It means that your services are good and respected and clients want to use your salon.

Even if the **Saturation Cycle** occurs i.e. many competitors, you would have to be very resourceful to maintain your business without devaluing treatments by unnecessary price cutting.

This is the time to use your skills and put your reserve plans into action.

You might:
- expand, take on a new service;
- an additional product.

This is the value of promotions.

Regular promotions bring in regular clients and can attract new ones.

Your business is founded on:
- client care;
- excellent service.

Clients that are **satisfied** don't usually want to shop around in the beauty trade, not if **personal care** has been your major concern. There will always be a trade of passers-by but it is your regular clients that are your stability. It is on this structure that you build.

If your forecast shows a particular **low** period ask yourself why? You have an annual business so you must maintain an annual trade. What will keep your clients visiting regularly? Could a promotion help? Could a special seasonal voucher help after an expensive holiday period? These vouchers may be accumulated to spend for treatments or to reduce the cost of a treatment.

Try it

spend a voucher
save a client
secure your booking for your 'low' time

Recession is another business stage which often comes before the **decline cycle**. The **Decline Cycle**, you should not reach if you are managing a business well.

It means that there is
- no growth;
- few sales;
- no profits.

Recession on the other hand can affect most businesses. It is like being in the decline stage and for some businesses that would be the next step down the ladder.

Recession should be seen as an opportunity to test, develop and use all your business and marketing skills.

Recession means that there is little or no growth in industry, on a national scale, and consequently in prosperity because the country is experiencing financial problems.

The problems are then passed from:

large businesses
to small businesses
to the consumer

It is time to consider the essential services your clients need and to develop new ones. If you have space you may consider:

RENT-A-SPACE

You may rent part of your salon to other professional people who want an outlet for their services. Perhaps they can no longer afford to run their own establishment or they are just starting up. All of you can benefit from the business. Services that you might consider for rent-a-space could include:
- osteopaths;
- hairdressers;
- colour analysis;
- chiropodists;
- nutritionists.

This

brings new clients to the salon
additional treatments
gives you the opportunity to present your services
uses space that may not have been fully used.

You will still want to budget your money carefully. Clients are still going to have treatments but they will be more selective because they are cutting-back. **Create** economy sales packages. See what your client **needs** and offer her additional **benefits** by introducing a different economy treatment each month.

Clients will be looking for bargains especially for services that they **need**. Perhaps they have a friend who needs your **essential services** as well. An inexpensive promotional evening to show the essential services that you offer could be just the attraction at this time.

check out your clients
their needs
their colleagues and friends.

Listen to your clients. Use your questionnaire and suggestion box and any other method that you feel will help you understand their needs.

What would your clients want as a freebie?
What are the essential treatments they need?

Tailor make your packages according to needs.

REMEMBER

a satisfied client speaks well of you
|
speaks well of the salon
|
recommends you/the salon
|
generates new business
|
returns to the salon

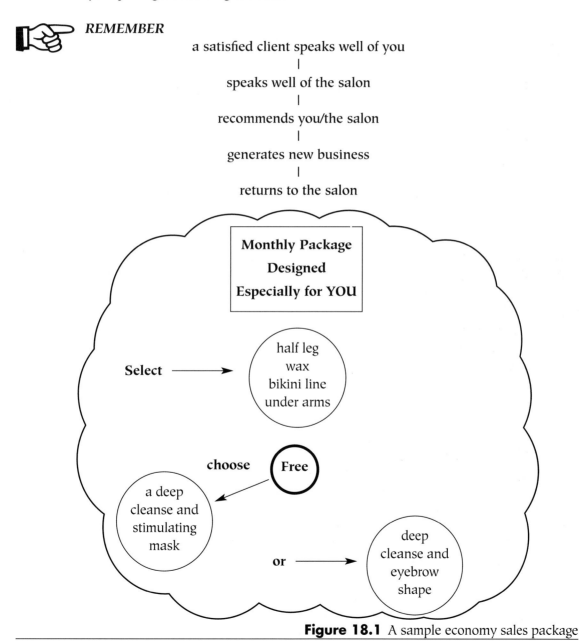

Figure 18.1 A sample economy sales package

ADAPT TO SURVIVE/EXPAND

If your business has been built on good foundations and you have kept a careful record of business accounts, disasters should not occur:

lack of experience

|

poor management

|

inadequate resources

are some of the reasons why businesses collapse. *Never* ignore cash flow problems or a drop in business. Obtain advice from your accountant or bank manager if there are financial problems. **Bankruptcy** occurs when a business **cannot pay its debts**.

A **court** declares a **business** or an **individual bankrupt** on the grounds that it/you is **insolvent**, which means the business is **unable to pay its debts**. A **receiver** is then appointed to take over the affairs of the **insolvent** business/individual.

If you are doubtful about your business, then there are various options open to you. You could:
- sell the business or the lease;
- clear your stock.

Before things get too serious, use your skills and adapt to survive. Use rent-a-space to develop business or to change the face of your present business. The most important factor is to assess what is needed and see if you can supply it.

If you develop your business well and always maintain business accounts, you should be able to take preventative measures in the early stages of any problem:

> Cutting back early saves cutting off later.

Self Assessments and Activities

1 Consider how a beauty business could be successful during a recession.

2 Design an economy treatment package to help your business and your client. State how you would promote this economically.

3 Explain how a business becomes insolvent.

4 Explain briefly how bankruptcy can be avoided.

5 List ten points to show how your salon could adapt in order to survive in business.

6 Your employer becomes insolvent – describe the action you should take.

7 Suggest 10 ways of how your salon could adapt in order to survive in business when you are in the saturation cycle.

8 Prepare a short questionnaire to give to your clients in order to test your services for:

a) quality

b) cost

c) personal service

9 In order to send out a mail shot you will need to plan the task. List all the preparation you will need to do until you finally post the letters.

CHAPTER 19

Creating an excellent salon

OBJECTIVES

Business development is founded on an awareness of the customer's needs, a knowledgeable approach to services and products and an awareness of business competitors. Business strategy comes from observing, listening and acting upon your findings, targeting your needs and promoting your business accordingly.

Business development is dependent on maintaining and improving the quality of work, and this means on-going staff training and the development and acquisition of new skills.

Creating an excellent salon means that you have professionally established good foundations in many aspects of business and that you must continue to develop, change and discover and maintain Personal Peak Performance.

You will no doubt use many forms of marketing and promotions throughout your business life. Initially, and ultimately, the main point is to acquire business. And once you have acquired business you must keep it. Building and keeping clientele is about:

> service: personal attention and being aware of your clients' needs.

You need to be:

knowledgeable about your services

|

knowledgeable about your products

|

aware of your clients – their likes and dislikes

|

aware of your competitors

|

the 'best' for service and personal care

TRAINING AND DEVELOPMENT

Most salon owners realise the necessity for on-going training and a progressive business will consider training as a **key factor** to improve salon standards and procedures.

Whether you have a large establishment or a small salon you will probably give some in-house training. You will also send your staff to particular training courses and annual exhibitions to ensure that they keep up-to-date with latest professional and technical skills and business techniques.

Staff training

Regular training means staff feel:

- confident and
- competent

and able to cope with their position.

When you decide on a training session:

- it may be because your observations have shown that there is a general weakness in one particular area;
- you need to advise your staff of a new development.

So how will you prepare for your session? You will need to decide:

- how long the session will last;
- how many people you will train;
- what skills you will demonstrate;
- how you will demonstrate them;
- what visual aids you will need;
- what staff participation you will expect;
- how you will test/evaluate staff's performance.

If you start with these few points you will be able to develop a plan for training.

Your structure will guide your development. You will then plan each section adequately and not spend too much time on one part.

You will need to consider:
- **your voice**: this needs to be varied if you want to maintain your staff's attention;
- **the way you stand**: this needs to be a definite presentation of self;
- **your body language**;
- **your visual language**.

Your eyes and body movements are important in conveying your interest in the subject and your audience. Regular movement of the eyes from one person to another sends the message that you are delivering your talk to each person. **Positive** open gestures with your hands or arms suggests warmth and breadth of communication.

A rigid stare, a totally upright, fixed body with no hand movements conveys a closed unfriendly message.

 REMEMBER
- your approach;
- your enthusiasm;
- your tone of voice;
- your information;

are the tools of your success in delivering a successful training session.

Training staff initiative

You may offer a creative training session developing staff initiative. **Developing staff awareness** in the business environment is vital to success. Staff need to understand the importance of their particular roles in the structure.

Teach your staff to be trainers if they show the initiative.

Staff training for sales

Regular training and incentive schemes form the basis for a good selling environment:

Selling practices

When you are supervising the staff in selling you will need to make several observations about **how**:

- the sale is started;
- the client's needs are identified;
- the therapist responds;
- the product or service is sold;
- **link selling can be encouraged**;
- the sale is transacted (closed).

Your role is **twofold**:

- **you are supervising a member of staff**
- **you are ensuring the client is satisfied.**

Ask yourself – **did the therapist**:

- smile, look relaxed, look interested, speak confidently;
- find out what the client needed;
- explain how the product or service would benefit the client;
- link the sale to other products or services;
- note when the client was considering, thinking, nodding her head **(buying signs)** and then **wait** patiently;
- respond as soon as the client said 'yes';
- **process the sale** – take payment and record the information on the client's record card or file;
- smile and thank the client?

If the therapist missed any of these **basic points** then further training is needed.

You will need to **offer advice** or set up role play situations so that the therapist can develop **confidence** and **competence**.

Regular product training

- keeps the therapist up to date;
- stimulates selling skills.

Services

Learning new services means that the staff can offer a greater variety of treatments.

This means that:

- staff learn new skills and refresh existing ones
- staff have greater job satisfaction.

Incentive schemes

You should monitor **incentive schemes** for your staff.

Incentive schemes are a good way to:

- promote more sales;
- reward staff for their effort.

Staff are generally paid a high commission on sales products and a lower one on services.

A high-priced product will earn good sales commission for the employee so that she/he has a good incentive to sell the product.

Many businesses offer incentive schemes, such as a monthly chart recording the individual employee's sales. The winner for the month then receives a bonus or prize. This can be a very good way to gain extra perks and can encourage individuals to perfect their selling skills.

You will need to assess when a scheme needs changing.

 REMEMBER
You are working with the other employees:
- **listen** to their comments
- **note** their likes or dislikes
- if the system is not functioning well **note the changes** early
- adjust the system.

In-house weekly training

Regular training might include:
- video training/new techniques;
- maintaining a good self image;
- improving telephone communication;
- promoting a new service;
- update on handling complaints;
- fire evacuation;
- new products;
- evaluating sales performance.

New skill development could focus on:

- marketing and sales;
- supervisory and management skills;
- new therapies.

Leading companies and banks often talk to groups/businesses as part of their service. Your business could benefit from their expertise. Banking, accounting and financial planning services are some of the topics they will talk about.

The importance of on-going training and maintaining high standards will be reflected in a growing industry and developing business.

MAINTAINING AND DEVELOPING BUSINESS

The personal touch

The beauty business is founded on the **personal approach**. Clients can afford to be selective and some are willing to travel miles to receive the sort of attention and service they require.

REMEMBER
Build your business by being better than your competitors

- see the want;
- fill the need;
- reap the benefit.

You can **never** be complacent. Carry out continual client monitoring:

- encourage your clients to complete a monthly questionnaire;
- evaluate your clients comments;
- consider their likes and dislikes;

about

- the salon
- the services
- the staff
- ask if they recommend your services

and so on . . .

Good business strategy and business development come from:

 observing
listening
acting upon your findings
being flexible
seeing the need for change

The beauty industry produces new products and treatments at a rapid pace.

 *REMEMBER*

Clients like good service
reliable treatments

You must be discerning. Not all clients want new treatments all the time. Excellent therapists performing established treatments give your clients confidence, create well-being and encourage them to return again and again.

Positive business results from:

regular custom
existing clients lead to
new clients

because successful salons are sought after salons.

An excellent salon is a successful salon when you have considered all the major sections.

Staff

|

Standards

|

Services
Satisfied Clients

|

Self

Happy well trained staff create a harmonious working environment.

Staff meetings held weekly or better still, daily.

       keep staff well-informed
       ensure **staff support** is available
       mean you work as a team

so no one struggles or feels alone. You will always need to exercise all your leadership skills (see page 25) to maintain the right balance.

Contented staff will want to maintain high standards that is:

personal standards
|
salon standards
.|
cleanliness
|
tidiness
|
attractiveness

This is then reflected in the **professional services** that they offer. Naturally therapists will earn a good income with good incentives and be successful. Through good service and high standards your staff will be successful and you will have satisfied clients.

In the 'best' environment everyone will want to keep it that way. Always attending to details so that the salon looks bright, fresh and stimulating to the enquirer and the employee. Your salon will develop and grow with:

effective management
|
skilled efficient staff
|
excellent services
a constant business and client awareness
|
market research

And so to you the salon-owner. Your success can only be measured by your self. i.e.

Self-image
and
Self-esteem

Successful managers/owners are **positive people** who have

    a high self esteem know where they are coming from and where they are going
    they appreciate their skills and they encourage others to do the same
    they are self-motivating with no self-imposed limits
    they visualise success and they achieve it

Maintaining Personal Peak Performance in your salon is very important so developing your own career aims must continue.

In order to achieve excellence you must give it in every aspect of your work. Meeting people's needs means that they will want to come and meet you. Your reputation must be highly prized. Your salon must be widely known (see Marketing page 164). Your salon must be seen to be a prominent feature in your town. This takes time to establish and time to develop but solid foundations lead to growth, expansion and success.

Self Assessment and Activities

1 List five ways that you could find out about your clients' needs.

2 List ten ways you could improve upon your personal service to your clients.

3 Design a promotion for introducing new clients to your salon.

4 Give five examples to show how you would expand your existing clientele.

5 Design an on-going training plan for three staff so that your salon and your staff will benefit.

6 Plan a promotion to encourage new clientele to try your salon.

7 'Personal service' is important. Justify this and suggest how it could be improved.

8 'Postgraduate training is vital to salon success' – comment on this statement.

9 Prepare a one hour in-house training session for 6 members of staff, on 'handling client complaints'.

10 Plan an in-house training programme schedule for 12 one hour weekly sessions.

Glossary

AHA peeling   alpha, hydroxy acids are fruit acids used in some skin care peeling products

annual percentage rate (APR)   The annual rate of interest charged on a loan. The APR must be clearly stated by all lenders – banks, building societies, finance companies.

appraisal   To monitor an employee's performance.

appraissee   The person being appraised.

appraiser   The person conducting the appraisal.

balance sheet   A statement of the assets and liabilities of a business at a particular point in time.

bankruptcy   A court can declare an individual or business bankrupt on the grounds that it is insolvent (unable to pay its debts). The affairs of the insolvent person or business are put in the hands of an official receiver.

body language   non-verbal communication e.g. facial expression

business plan   A plan which shows your business ideas and activities in detail and predicts the expectations of the business for the year. A business plan is necessary to support an application for a loan.

capital   The total assets of an individual or business, that is, cash, property and other assets.

capital investment   An investment of money into a business for equipment that is permanent or semi-permanent.

cash book   A daily record of payments and receipts.

cash flow forecast   An estimate of a business's cash incomings and cash outgoings over a particular period, for example, six months to a year.

closed question   a question that only warrants yes or no for an answer

code of ethics   a code of practice based on the professional standards of behaviour

contra-action   an adverse reaction to a substance (product) or treatment

contract of employment   A written or unwritten legally binding agreement between an employer and employee.

contra-indication   a reason why a treatment must not be given

credit note   A supplier issues this when there has been an overpayment.

creditor   An individual or company to whom money is owed, for example, suppliers and the bank.

current account   An account with a bank that enables you to write cheques for payment of your bills.

current assets   Assets in the balance sheet which can easily be converted into cash, such as stock.

current liabilities Liabilities in the balance sheet which show money owed, for example, a bank overdraft. These are short-term debts.

database electronic filing system held on a computer

debit note This is issued by a supplier when the salon owner owes money.

debtor An individual or a firm that owes you money.

delivery note When goods have been received by a salon, a detailed note will accompany them from the supplier.

Department of Social Security (DSS) Government department that deals with social benefits – National Insurance, sickness and maternity.

deposit account A savings account with a bank that enables you to deposit money and pays you interest.

egress a way out of an area

e-mail electronic mail sent by telecommunication through a computer

employer's liability insurance This insurance protects the employer from any claims made by an employee injured on the premises.

exempt goods Goods or services which have been declared exempt from VAT (VAT is not payable on them).

fax a method of sending documents or black and white photographs via telephone lines to another fax machine

fixed assets Property or assets in a balance sheet which cannot quickly be converted into cash, for example, freehold properties and fixtures.

fixtures and fittings Equipment that is included in the sale of a business. This is usually itemised in an inventory.

franchise A licence to trade in the name of another company, usually for an initial premium and regular commission on sales.

gross profit The profit a business makes before deducting operating expenses, such as overheads and depreciation on equipment.

input VAT This is paid on your purchases if you are registered for VAT.

insolvency This is when a firm or individual can no longer pay debts as they fall due.

Internet a world-wide collection of information available through computers

interpersonal skills these are people skills – vital for good communication

invoice A bill for goods supplied on credit stating the goods supplied, the date they were supplied, the cost, VAT if applicable and the supplier's terms.

job description/job specification A written summary of an employee's title and tasks.

lease An agreement for a firm or individual when renting (leasing) property for a stated period of time. The individual or firm is the tenant or lessee. The landlord is the lessor.

leasehold property A tenant holds property under a lease – the tenant does not own the property.

ledger A system which uses double-entry bookkeeping.

liabilities Amounts owed by a business to others.

limited company   When two or more persons own a company. They are the shareholders. The limited company may be private or public.

link selling   selling products of the same range which complement each other

manufacturer   A company who makes a product or equipment.

market research   Researching an area, service or product in order to find out information.

National Insurance (NI)   This is the national scheme for paying for state benefits. Premiums are weekly or monthly and are based on wages or salaries paid. It is the employer's responsibility to deduct NI and to pay the premiums to the Inland Revenue.

net pay   This is the 'take home' pay after deductions have been made.

net profit   This is the profit of a business after all expenses and deductions have been made. Tax is payable on this.

open question   a question which requires a longer answer than just yes or no

output VAT   This is charged on goods and services if you are registered for VAT.

overdraft   when a bank gives extended credit on a current account

overheads   The everyday operating costs of running a business.

partnership   A business association of between two and 20 persons.

pay advice slip   Details of gross pay and relevant deductions to arrive at net pay. Employers are required to issue this.

Pay As You Earn (PAYE)   The employer is responsible for deducting NI and income tax from employees' pay.

personal allowance   The amount an individual is entitled to earn before paying tax.

planning permission   Legal permission must be obtained from the local authority in order to change the use of a property or to change its structure.

product liability   This insurance protects the retailer against claims resulting from products which are not the responsibility of the manufacturer.

professional indemnity insurance   insurance for named persons which protect them from claims made by clients in the event of personal injury as a result of a treatment

profit and loss   A record of the profit (or loss) made by a business over a stated period of time.

public liability insurance   This insurance protects the retailer if a member of the public is injured on the premises.

purchase order   A form that is used to buy products from another company.

recession   When there is no growth in industry on a national scale.

risk assessment   an assessment of risks associated with chemical products or work place

Schedule D tax   This is payable on the net profit of your business when your accounts have been submitted to the Inland Revenue.

sole proprietor/trader   A person who owns and runs a business on her/his own.

statement   A written reminder of outstanding amounts owed (often monthly).

stock   Goods held for re-selling.

stock-take   This is required annually for your accounts and it means that the stock must be counted and valued.

stock turnover   This is when stock is sold quickly (turned over) and cash is available.

trading account   A summary of sales for a period, usually a year, together with the costs of sales for the same period showing the resulting gross profit.

trial balance   A list of debit and credit balances taken from an accounts ledger.

value added tax (VAT)   A tax on most goods and services in the UK.

VAT return   A form which records details of VAT paid or received by a retailer – it must be completed quarterly and sent to HM Customs and Excise.

vendor   The same as seller, for example, of a property.

wages record book   A record of all wages paid by an employer and required for accounting purposes.

web site   a collection of electronic documents available through computers

wholesaler/supplier   One who buys goods in bulk and sells in smaller quantities to retailers.

working capital   the money that is required to run the business on a daily basis

Further reading

Atkinson, P E, *Achieving Results Through Time Management*, Pitman, 1988

Brewer, Roy, *Do-it-Yourself Advertising*, Kogan Page, 1991

Business Checklists: Small Business Management, Hodder & Stoughton, 1999

Collins, Helen, *Human Resource Management: Personnel, Policies and Procedures*, Hodder & Stoughton, 1993

Cook, Sarah, *Customer Care*, Kogan Page, 1992

Cox, Roger, *Retailing*, Macdonald and Evans, 1993

Davies, Barry and Davies, Eric, *Successful Marketing in a Week 2nd Edition*, Hodder & Stoughton, 1999

Health and Safety Executive, *Essentials of Health and Safety at Work*, HMSO, 1990

Maitland, Iain, *The Business Planner*, Butterworth–Heinemann, 1992

Maitland, Iain, *Successful Business Plans in a Week 2nd Edition*, Hodder & Stoughton, 1998

Mallory, Charles, *Direct Mail*, Kogan Page, 1992

Morris, M J, *Starting a Successful Small Business*, 2nd edn, Kogan Page, 1992

Pullen, Max, *Business Cash Books Made Easy*, Kogan Page, 1992

Rogers, Len, *Barclays Guide to Marketing*, Blackwell, 1990

Secrett, Malcolm, *Successful Budgeting in a Week*, Hodder & Stoughton, 1993

Treacy, Declan, *Successful Time Management in a Week*, Hodder & Stoughton, 1993

Whittaker, Maxine, Forsythe-Conroy, Debbie and Ifould, Judith, *Beauty Therapy: the Basics for NVQ Level 3*, Hodder & Stoughton, 1999

Williams, David, *Running Your Own Business*, Longman, 1990

Woodcock, Clive, *The Guardian Guide to Running a Small Business*, Kogan Page, 1988

Relevant acts and regulations

Consumer Protection Act 1987
Control of Substances Hazardous to Health Act (COSHH) 1989
COSHH Regulations 1992
Cosmetic Products Regulations 1989
Data Protection Act 1984
Disability Discrimination Act 1995
Electricity at Work Regulations 1989–1992
Employer's Liability Act 1969
Employment Protection (Consolidation) Act 1978
Employment Rights Act 1996
Environmental Protection Act 1990
Equal Pay Act 1970–1983
EU Regulations 1992 (six pack)
    1. Management of Health and Safety at Work Regulations 1992
    2. Workplace (Health, Safety and Welfare) Regulations 1992
    3. Provisions and Use of Work Equipment Regulations 1992
    4. Personal Protective Equipment (PPE) at Work Regulations 1992
    5. Health and Safety (Display Screen Equipment) Regulations 1992
    6. Manual Handling Operations Regulations 1992
Local Government (Miscellaneous Provisions) Act 1982 (Local Authority Licensing)
Misrepresentation Act 1967
Race Relations Act 1976
Re-Sale Price Acts 1964, 1976
Reporting of Injuries, Diseases and Dangerous Occurrences Regulations 1995 (RIDDOR)
Sexual Discrimination Act 1975–1986
Social Security Act 1996
Supply of Goods and Services Act 1994
The Cheque Act 1992
Trade Descriptions Act 1968, 1972
Woolf Report 1999
Working Time Regulations 1998

Associations

Association of Reflexologists
27 Old Gloucester Street
London WC1N 3XX

British Association of Beauty Therapy and Cosmetology Ltd
2A Tudor Way
Hillingdon
Uxbridge UB10 9AB

British Association of Skin Camouflage
25 Blackhorse Drive
Silkstone Common
Nr Barnsley
South Yorkshire S75 4SD

International Aestheticiennes
Bache Hall
Bache Hall Estate
Chester CH2 2BR

International Federation of Aromatherapists
Department of Continuing Education
Royal Masonic Hospital
Ravenscourt Park
London W6 0TN

The Federation of Holistic Therapists
3rd Floor
Eastleigh House
Upper Market Street
Eastleigh SO50 9FD

Independent Professional Therapists International
58A Bridgegate
Retford
Nottinghamshire DN22 7U2

International Society of Professional Aromatherapists
Hinkley and District Hospital and Health Care
The Annexe
Mount Road
Hinkley
Leicestershire LE10 1AE

The Guild of Professional Beauty Therapists
Guild House
PO Box 310
Derby DE23 9BR

Sources of information

Advertising Standards Authority
Brook House
2–16 Torrington Place
London WC1E 7HN

Association of British Insurers
Aldermary House
Queen Street
London EC4N 1TT

British Franchise Association
Franchise Chambers
Thames View
Newtown Road
Henley-on-Thames
Oxfordshire RG9 1HE

British Insurance Brokers Association
BIBA House
14 Bevis Marks
London EC3A 7NT

Companies Registration Office:
England and Wales
Companies House
Crown Way
Maindy
Cardiff CF4 3UZ

Northern Ireland
Dept of Economic Development
64 Chichester Street
Belfast BT1 4JX

Scotland
102 George Street
Edinburgh EH2 3DJ

Customs & Excise
New Kings Beam House
22 Upper Ground
London SE1 9PS

Department of Employment
Caxton House
Tothill Street
London SW1H 9NF

Department of the Environment
Eland House
Bressenden Place
London SW1E 5DU

England and Wales: see Scottish Division or DOE Scotland

Department of the Environment (DOE)
(Northern Ireland)
Town and Country Planning Service
Commonwealth House
35 Castle Street
Belfast TR1 1GU

Environmental Health Officers are employed by local authorities – telephone numbers will be in 'Business and Services Directory' or 'Thomson Local Directory'.

Equal Opportunities Commission
Overseas House
Quay Street
Manchester M3 3HN

Health and Safety Executive (HSE)
Rose Court
Southwark Bridge Road
London SE1 9HF

Scottish Business in the Community
Eagle Star House
25 St Andrews Square
Edinburgh EH2 1AF

Scottish Industry Department (IDS)
Sandyford Road
Paisley
Glasgow G2 6AT

Recruitment

Recruitment Services
The Guild of Professional Beauty Therapists (see Associations)
Rosemary Hadley Employment Agency
Hamilton House
1 Temple Avenue
London EC4 V0HA

Beauty Recruitment Plus (Worldwide)
Email: BRPSales@aol.com

Advertising

Thomson Directories
Thomson House
296 Farnborough Road
Farnborough
Hampshire GU14 7NU

Yellow Pages
Email: eypsales@yellowpages.co.uk

Magazines

Hairdressers' Journal/Health & Beauty Salon
Quadrant House
The Quadrant
Sutton
Surrey SM2 5AS

Professional Beauty (LNE)
Fairfax House
461–465 North End Road
Fulham
London SW6 1NZ

For Awarding Bodies information, refer to page 10.

Organisations you should know

The Office of Fair Trading (OFT)

This organisation is set up by the Government to protect consumers interests as well as traders.

It issues information and a variety of codes of practice to encourage trade associations to improve their standards. It can prosecute traders who break the Law.

The Consumer's Association

The Association carries out research into:

■ the quality of consumer products;
■ the standard of services.

It campaigns for consumer rights.

It publishes the magazine *Which*.

Environmental Health and Trading Standards (EHTS)

The EH Department investigate the quality of food and hygiene and may close a business which fails to comply with regulations. The TS Officers are employed by Local Authorities to investigate complaints brought by consumers (refer TS Dept.).

Trading Standards Department

This organisation has Trading Standards officers who investigate complaints relating to:

■ misleading offers;
■ inaccurate weight and measures;

Consumers Association

This Association is concerned with consumer rights. It strives to maintain that prices are not too high and that services are a good quality.

Advertising Standards Authority (ASA)

This organisation is independent. Its purpose is to ensure that all advertisements are legal and not misleading. The ASA produces particular guidelines for different companies. There are established guidelines for the promotion of Beauty Products.

National Consumer Council

This council represents the consumer in disputes or problems relating to government departments.

Citizen's Advice Bureau

This organisation offers advice on a number of matters. Its main function is to mediate in disputes between consumers and organisations.

British Standards Institution (BSI)

This organisation sets the minimum standards in business and industry. It is funded by the Government and voluntary donations. Its common mark is the BSI Kitemark, which denotes that a manufactured product has reached the standards specified by the BSI in safety, durability and quality.

Useful Addresses

Advisory Conciliation Arbitration Service (ACAS)
Clifton House
83–117 Euston Road
London NW1 2RB

Association of British Chambers of Commerce
Manning House
22 Carlisle Place
London SW1P 1JA

Association of Independent Business
38 Bow Lane
London EC4M 9AY

British Computer Society
Specialists Group Liaison
1 Stamford Street
Swindon
SN1 1HJ

Business Names Registration PLC
Somerset House
Temple Street
Birmingham
B2 5DN

British Technology Group
10 Fleet Place
Limeburner Road
London EC4M 7SB

Business in the Community
8 Stratton Street
Mayfair
London W1X 6AH

Confederation of British Industry (CBI)
Centrepoint
103 New Oxford Street
London WC1A 1DU

Contributions Agency
Self Employment Group
DSS Longbenton
Newcastle-upon-Tyne
NE98 1YX
www.dss.gov.uk/co/

Department of Social Security (DSS)
Richmond House
79 Whitehall
London SW1A 2NS
See local 'phone book under 'Benefits Agency/Social Security'

Department of Trade and Industry (DTI)
1 Victoria Street
London SW1H 0ET

National Federation of Small Businesses
32 Orchard Road
Lytham St Annes
Lancashire FY8 1NY

Office of The Data Protection Registrar
Wycliffe House
Water Lane
Wilmslow
Cheshire SK9 5AF

Scottish Enterprise
120 Bothwell Street
Glasgow G2 7JP

Suppliers

EQUIPMENT AND PRODUCTS

Carlton Professional
Taylor Reeson
Commerce Way
Lancing
Sussex BN15 8TA

Depilex
2 Marsh Lane
Nantwich
Cheshire CW5 5HH

Dermatologica
Caxton House
Randalls Way
Leatherhead
Surrey KT22 7TW

Ellisons
Crondal Road
Exhall
Coventry CV7 9NH
Tel: 0203 361619
Fax: 0203 644010

HOF – Le Club
The Grange
Beeston Green
Sandy
Bedfordshire SG19 1PG

Medex
Medex House
53–53A Belswains Lane
Hemel Hempstead
Hertfordshire HP3 9PP
Tel: 0442 249797

Susan Molyneux
9 King Street
Cheltenham
Gloucestershire
Tel: 0242 570515

SALON WEAR

Buttercups
26A Powerscourt
Townhouse Centre
Dublin

Ellisons
Crondal Road
Exhall
Coventry CV7 9NH

Figaro
466A Green Lanes
Palmers Green
London
N13 5PA

Florence Ruby
Caddick Road
Knowsley Industrial Park South
Merseyside L34 9HP

Index